"I meet a lot of high school and college students who profess to be Christians but have never actually read through the Bible. They confess little knowledge of the Bible and don't know how to answer basic questions about the faith. Some of these students attend church youth groups or to go Christian schools. As a pastor, and as one who often speaks to students, I have longed for a book to give to students, parents, teachers, and youth leaders. I want to see a generation of disciple-makers, but before we unleash these students as young disciple-makers, they must be trained in the essentials of the faith. My good friend Todd von Helms has provided a much needed resource for all who share this kind of burden. I wholeheartedly recommend it."

Tony Merida, Pastor, Imago Dei Church, Raleigh, NC, Author of *Ordinary: How to Turn the World Upside Down*

"The chapter on the Bible is extremely well-written, concise (for a huge topic), expertly organized, and persuasive. I will use it as a guide for myself."

Grant Wacker, Professor Emeritus of Christian History, Duke University

"Dr. von Helms has the gift of taking difficult topics and making them understandable in a way that transforms one's thinking. This book will have a cross generational appeal and be an excellent resource for those in academia and the Church."

Adam Wright, President, Dallas Baptist University

"Given his exceptional credentials and vast experience, I cannot think of anyone better suited to help address the myriad challenges facing today's youth and college students."

Hon. Mark Martin, Chief Justice of the Supreme Court of North Carolina (ret.), Dean and Professor, Regent Law School

"This book provides a very direct engagement of what are some of the most challenging topics and ideas that many of us have never dealt with in a deep and meaningful way. It is rich, practical, and powerful."

Brigadier General Tim Gibson, President of the King's College, New York City

"I've watched Todd von Helms engage students for many years. It's remarkable. Few authors have both academic credibility and the ability to engage students. There is no one more suited to write a book like this. While this book is a challenge to skeptics and affirming for believers, it should be essential reading for all students before they leave f̶ ̶c̶o̶l̶l̶e̶g̶e̶ and their respective vocations."

Dr. Steven Smith, Senior Pastor, Ir̶ sas

D0911093

"From years of experience working with students and young people, Todd von Helms offers a much-needed book for those raised in the church who have never had the opportunity to address the hard and inevitable questions put to our faith. I am grateful for his irenic spirit and conversational tone, while still facing head on the more academic-like questions in a down-to-earth kind of way."

Fr. Wes Gristy, Rector, All Saints Anglican Church, Jackson, Tennessee

"We can no longer expect to send our sons and daughters from Sunday school to college without a serious jolt to their faith. They're leaving home unequipped to answer a barrage of modern challenges to beliefs they've held dear, but haven't held deep. Now there's an accessible book that will help young Christians gain a firmer grasp of what and why they believe."

Peggy Wehmeyer, journalist, former ABC News religion correspondent

"Here is a book that was sorely needed! Too many Christians, especially teenagers, are turning away from Christianity because they have unresolved doubts about God and His Word. The church and the Christian academy have too often shied away from addressing these uncertainties, but Todd von Helms has not. He has taken the offensive position and produced a book that provides sound and satisfying solutions to the most pressing theological questions of our day. Through it all, readers of Before You Leave will be equipped and encouraged to know, trust, and proclaim the God who created them for his glory. May the Lord bless everyone who reads it!"

Nicholas Harris, Principal, Berean Christian High School, Walnut Creek, California

"This thoughtful book gives wisdom for parents, Catholic and Protestant alike, who are seeking to help their children form a strong, intellectual foundation for their walk with Jesus. It is also a clear, helpful guide to students navigating how to be witnesses to their faith in an increasingly secularized culture."

Jake Rodgers, Principal, Sacred Heart Cathedral School, Knoxville, Tennessee

"I commend this book to you because I think it will help you to explore the essential questions that we are all asking, both inside the church, and outside the church."

Blake Holmes, Watermark Church, Campus Pastor & Director of the Watermark Institute, Dallas, Texas

"The scope and breadth of this book is an amazing resource for you to address questions about the Bible, prayer, the supernatural realm, and what science reveals about the place of God in the universe."

Mike Strauss, Professor of Physics, University of Oklahoma, CERN Project researcher, Geneva, Switzerland, Reasons to Believe visiting scholar

"In *Before You Leave*, Todd von Helms deals with hard questions without backing down, while at the same time he communicates with a gracious posture and exhorts his readers to do the same. This is truly a book full of grace and truth!"

Rev. David Billingslea, Campus Minister, RUF-International

"This book is so valuable because it addresses the topics most people do not talk about. It is important to confront and decide what we think about difficult subjects like death, hell, and the devil, because scripture addresses each of these topics. This book also helps us to understand how the Bible came to be, which in turn strengthens our ability to bear witness to the background of scripture, and to scripture's authority, with people who may have only a simplistic or stereotypical view of Bible-believing Christians."

Warren Smith, Professor of Historical Theology, Duke University

"Before You Leave is a powerful appeal to Christian high school students who are headed to college. Von Helms encourages them to stand strong in the Christian faith, embrace the full span of the Bible's teaching, and to be witnesses for Christ in one of the most difficult arenas in American life—the university. Highly recommended."

Bruce Riley Ashford, Provost of Southeastern Baptist Theological Seminary and author of *Letters to an American Christian.*

"This book allowed me as a parent not to be afraid to talk about difficult topics and walk alongside my teenagers. I'm so glad I had this book as a tool to guide me along in the journey as a mom, wife, and Christian in the workforce."

Madison Lane, #1 rated radio host, 96.1 BBB Raleigh-Durham, North Carolina

"This book provides an in-depth and yet accessible treatment of key areas that are essential foundations for being prepared to give a defense for the Christian faith in today's post truth cultural context. I believe it will not only be an indispensable aid for students, parents and ministry leaders, but also become a go-to resource for any serious Christ-follower."

Ray Williams, Fellowship Church, Little Rock, Founder & CEO City Church Network

"This book addresses the primary classical apologetical questions and gives the reader a solid understanding of some very important issues including how we got the Bible, challenges from atheists, understanding evil, the devil and hell, and practicing the spiritual discipline of prayer. My favorite component of the book is the introduction of the reader to seemingly countless great men and women of the faith as examples throughout the book – some more common like C.S. Lewis, Charles Spurgeon and Jonathan Edwards, but many more lesser known saints of the faith whom the reader will find equally engaging. Von Helms doesn't seek to answer every question, but readers will find that when they are finished with this book, they will have a solid foundation for the fundamental Christian faith and be ready to engage in meaningful and persuasive dialogue with others on important spiritual issues."

Dan Panetti, Prestonwood Christian Academy, Dallas, Texas

"The cultural current of secularism in the West is strong and pervasive. As a result, a significant percentage of American Christians have been swept away by it, leading to an emaciated form of faith that bears little resemblance to Jesus's teachings about what it means to be one of his followers. What may a person do? If you are a new believer or an older one who never grew out of spiritual infancy, Todd von Helms extends his hand to help you get up and get in the game. This book is a sort of primer that helps you navigate through some of the major discussions that challenge faith encountered by today's believer. Moreover, von Helms provides direction to help you climb to greater heights in your relationship with God."

Michael Licona, Associate Professor of Theology, Houston Baptist University

"Todd von Helms has done a great service to the church. By thoughtfully engaging common questions about the faith that most young people encounter as they move into adult life—and doing so from a standpoint informed by the Bible and historical theology—he has given her a resource by which she might take captive every thought to the obedience of Christ. I highly recommend this book to parents, youth groups, students heading off to college, and Christian schools."

Rev. Chris Stratton, Academic Dean, Pacifica Christian High School Orange County

"This book should be essential reading for college students, parents of college students, and for all of those involved in Christian higher education. Dr. von Helms is a wise and seasoned guide who skillfully navigates the morass of intellectual challenges to faith faced by the current generation of college students, leading the reader to ponder anew both the soundness and the beauty of historic Christianity. Highly recommended!"

Matt Hoehn, Director of Christian Thought, NC Study Center, Chapel Hill, NC

"Todd has a tremendous knack of writing clearly and in a way that draws you into the conversation. He respects your intellect, and takes you into the resources of scripture, divine revelation, and deep religious experience. This book should be drawn on to help people develop the intellectual, spiritual, and moral resources needed not just to survive, but to flourish."

Rev. Dr. William J. Abraham, Professor of Wesley Studies, Southern Methodist University

"Todd has created a great read, especially for high school and college students, for whom a better knowledge of religion in general and Christianity in particular is more important than ever. This book is good for those who do believe, those who don't believe, and for those who are not sure whether or what to believe. It is thought provoking for anyone, regardless of age."

Arkansas Democrat-Gazette

BEFORE YOU LEAVE

for COLLEGE,
CAREER, *and* ETERNITY

TODD VON HELMS

Before You Leave: For College, Career, and Eternity

Copyright © 2020 by Todd von Helms. All rights reserved.
Published by The King's College Press.

Scripture quotations taken from The Holy Bible, New International Version®
NIV®
Copyright © 1973 1978 1984 2011 by Biblica, Inc.TM
Used by permission. All rights reserved worldwide.

Cover photo: Chris Hendricks, Eden Anne Films

ISBN: 978-0-578-66098-1

For Hunter and Jake

CONTENTS

FOREWORD

Professor William J. Abraham
Southern Methodist University

Something needs to be done. Todd von Helms has done it!

Something needs to be done to help people move into a deeper and richer vision of the Christian faith. The reality is simple: For too long, we have remained satisfied with a faith that is an inch deep and a mile wide. This works, albeit inadequately, when Christians live in a culture that is still recognizably Christian. In that type of culture, we can assume a basis of Bible knowledge and get on with the business of Christian practice.

However, this kind of world was already under threat in the higher echelons of late nineteenth-century Europe. Now, even in Catholic Ireland where I once lived, the Christian scaffolding has vanished, all within one generation. When I was growing up in Ireland in the 1950s and 1960s, the writing was on the wall. Most of my friends readily abandoned the faith. The churches we inhabited are now a shadow of their previous selves, doing what they can to keep faith alive in a hostile environment. By the time I made it to university in Belfast, I could not find anyone to teach me philosophy of religion in a splendid philosophy department. I eventually turned to a wonderful, secular humanist, who had been blinded in the last days of World War II, and had become sincerely hostile to the claims of Christianity.

Gratefully, this professor happily took me on in a personal course to tackle some of the crucial intellectual questions that had been evoked by my conversion thanks to the love and labors of my local church.

I used to tell my students in North America that things were different in this part of the world. I laughed at the standard predictions of English sociologists who said the United States was simply a couple of generations behind Europe in the erosion of Christianity. I no longer laugh at this prediction. It is perfectly clear that we are indeed becoming more like Europe by the decade. We can leave for another occasion why this significant change has happened. The more important question is what we should do about a situation where people can now get training in how to create atheists, where feeble forms of Christianity are not worth disbelieving, and where loyal church members have no idea how to deal with the questions of their children and grandchildren. Something needs to be done, not the least of which is provide initial resources to our young people headed off to university where they are often the captive audience of professors all too ready to destroy what little faith they may have.

Consider our situation from another angle. Last year I received an email from a brilliant young Muslim who contacted me because he wanted to find out more about religion, especially about Christianity. I took him up on his request to meet; we now meet on a regular basis in my favorite French coffee shop. To say that he is brilliant is an understatement. I am morally certain that he will get into one of the top universities in the United States. Moreover, he knows the Koran by heart. He has already worked his way through most of the New Testament, and currently, as a matter of choice, he is working his way through the canonical sermons of John Wesley. He is a model of intelligence and grace. Compare his Muslim formation with formation in the "Kentucky Fried Christianity" that we meet so often in the church and in the culture.

Not surprisingly, many adult believers, not to speak of our young people, are woefully ignorant of the first principles of Christian teaching and practice. This splendid young Muslim already knows his own faith well enough to study a rival faith with confidence. No doubt he is exceptional. However, I would bet a month's salary that few equally intelligent young Christians would have a clue on how to handle his questions about and objections to Christianity. Something needs to be done before it is too late; we cannot afford to lose another generation.

Todd von Helms has provided exactly what we need to get started. He has already had an illustrious career teaching youth and college students—and now has hit on a surprising and effective strategy to tackle the challenges we face. Professional theologians have tended to take one of two courses of action. Some retreat into their own intellectual world and assume that there is little point in reaching out to those who need academic answers. Others rush to accommodate the faith to the fads and fashions of the hour. As Professor Bryan Wilson, an atheist sociologist at Oxford, remarked to me in personal conversation: "Some theologians are so worried about being kicked in the ditch by their critics that they jump in the ditch to avoid the anticipated pain." Todd von Helms has taken another tack: dive right into the deep issues that make a real difference in what we believe as a whole and that radically shape the kind of life we intend to live. But also, he does so in a way that takes seriously the difficulties in understanding and believing that occur naturally to people living in a world that is either hostile to the faith or has given up on embracing an industrial-strength version of the faith.

Todd von Helms clearly recognizes a basic principle of teaching and communication: tackle the big issues, and the small fries will take care of themselves. Most people can readily see through the throat-clearing, which we are tempted to take up before we get down to serious intellectual work. Von Helms avoids this by identifying the central issues that are needed to do justice to the real questions that arise. So he goes straight to work on questions about the Bible, the New Atheism, the devil, hell, and prayer. He does not evade the issues. He invites readers to bring their brains to the task, he includes suitable resources in the footnotes, and he ends with a raft of practical suggestions as to how to move forward.

Something needs to be done to give backbone to Christians, especially those young in the faith. Todd von Helms has done it with flair in this splendid volume.

INTRODUCTION

The message of Christianity is rather simple, but following Christ can be very challenging. For most believers, the journey starts during childhood. My earliest recollection of God was conveyed through the first line of a popular children's song: "Jesus loves me, this I know, for the Bible tells me so." Like many religious people, what I learned as a child determined my view of the Bible and how I related to God and others.

Much of my formal education was taught from a Christian perspective, and it was wonderful being surrounded by many like-minded people. I remember coaches at my public high school praying before and after games, as well as history teachers pointing out that our calendar proved that Jesus was the cornerstone upon which the church and modern civilization were built. Anything that occurred prior to the birth of Jesus was labeled BC (before Christ), whereas anything that occurred afterward was labeled AD, which is the abbreviation for *anno Domini*, a Latin term that means "the year of the Lord." Life was busy, and God was never far away. I remember going to church, and even hearing and seeing references to Jesus in our "lost," secular world, especially at Easter and Christmastime. I was enjoying the benefits and conveniences of cultural Christianity, and I didn't even know it.

Like many people who grow up as Christians in America, much of what I had learned went out the window during college. Although I believed the Bible and was ready to live out my faith, I was ill-prepared for the intellectual challenges that loomed on the collegiate horizon. During my first week of classes, I noticed that some of my professors and textbooks had opted to replace the traditional labels (BC and AD) with the abbreviations BCE (before common era) and CE (common era) as if to avoid any reference to Jesus Christ. Each week, I saw advertisements for dozens of religious groups, most of which I knew nothing about. Hanging out with atheists and those adhering to other religions caused me to question if what I believed was naïve, restrictive, or simply the product of my upbringing. Though I had been taught that no one could enter heaven except through faith in Jesus (John 14:6; Acts 4:12), my non-Christian friends just seemed way too nice and cool to end up in a place called hell. As the semester unfolded, my desire to share the Good News waned.

What really threw me for a loop was discovering that some of my "unchurched" friends knew more about the Bible than I did. It seemed that everywhere I turned, everything that I had learned about God was being challenged. I was completely blindsided by my literature and religious studies courses, as professors and classmates raised questions about the Bible that I could not answer. I began to wonder why the Christian leaders I knew and respected had ignored or failed to teach the many things I was now learning.

When I returned home to ask them about what my professors were teaching me, the responses were not helpful. Typically, I would hear, "You can't trust what that professor is telling you, for he doesn't know the Author of the Bible." One leader said, "Don't waste your time with stuff like that, for the devil is behind it!" Another said, "You shouldn't ask such questions. Instead, you really just need to have faith and believe that the Bible is perfect."

To my surprise, some of the well-meaning people I asked for advice said, "I don't know," or "I've never heard the questions you are posing." Those responses caused me to question if my mentors in the faith were versions of the caricatures that the critics were talking about—narrow-minded, biblically inept Christians. Though my church leaders loved me and were faithful in proclaiming the gospel and teaching from the Bible, some of them were ill-equipped to answer the particular questions that were challenging my faith. A few of my classmates ended up walking away from their faith, which drove me to know more about the challenges that were being posed.

In addition to being unprepared for the intellectual and spiritual challenges, more than anything, I just wanted to fit in. Most of my friends were just trying to make it to classes and find the next date, ballgame, or party. Experiencing such freedom can be both a blessing and a curse for college students. No one was telling us when to go to bed, get up in the morning, do our homework, or go to church. Because I was busy (and sometimes lazy), church became less of a priority, especially when it seemed to infringe upon my newfound liberties and desires. Even though I wanted to put God first, it seemed that very few had similar intentions. At times it felt like the only two choices were to run with the crowd or stand alone.

Recent studies have confirmed what I personally experienced and have observed for many years: Two of the loneliest segments of the American population can be those entering nursing homes and colleges.[1] The reality is that many students attempting to hold on to their childhood faith often feel isolated, and sometimes intimidated,

---

[1] https://www.acha.org/documents/ncha/NCHA-II_Spring_2018_Reference_Group_Executive_Summary.pdf
https://www.cigna.com/newsroom/news-releases/2018/new-cigna-study-reveals-loneliness-at-epidemic-levels-in-america A study conducted by CIGNA deemed college students (ages 18-22) as the "loneliest generation" in America. The aforementioned studies did not differentiate between religious and non-religious people.

especially when the ethos of their new environment tends to ignore, contradict, belittle, or resent their religious beliefs. Despite the valiant efforts of many wonderful local churches and parachurch ministries devoted to shaping the minds and hearts of students, college can be a difficult place for many people of faith.

While working with youth and college students over the past twenty years, a few things have become glaringly obvious. For starters, biblical illiteracy remains a problem, and most Christian students haven't thought too deeply about the Bible or Christianity. I cannot count the number of times I've heard students mention that they were unprepared to dialogue with those espousing differing views from their own. Reasons abound as to why this happens. Here's the main reason: Most Christians have never read the Bible cover to cover and therefore are unfamiliar with what it says. Until we have read our Bibles, we are unable to discern truth from falsehood. Theologian R.C. Sproul once stated, "It is safe to assume that more than eighty percent of Christians have not read the entire Bible."[2]

I've noticed that many parents and leaders are not expecting teenagers to learn the basics of the Bible and Christianity, much less deal with objections. Additionally, because some youth ministries and Christian schools don't tackle the difficult religious topics, many students don't feel comfortable talking about them. In the meantime, many of the questions and doubts are being addressed in places other than the church, such as college campuses, bars, best-selling books, websites, various media outlets, and the entertainment industry.

A couple of recent national surveys indicated that nearly 70 percent of university freshmen identified as religious, with the majority identifying as Christian[3]. But many of these students do not have a solid

[2] R.C. Sproul. *Knowing Scripture.* (Downers Grove, IL: InterVarsity Press, 1977), 18.
[3] https://heri.ucla.edu/cirp-freshman-survey/

understanding of the Bible. Though most teenagers believe they are ready for the challenges that await them, many are not. I remember feeling the same way, only to realize that my knowledge and understanding of the Bible were severely lacking. Exposure to new and differing ways of thinking is not the problem. Neither is doubting or questioning one's faith. The main problem is that many Christian students don't know what they believe or why they believe it, much less understand how to respond when their faith is challenged.

If students are not exposed to these issues, most will not be prepared to deal with them during college. I am convinced that a failure to expose young people (older people, too, for that matter) to the criticisms aimed at the Bible and Christianity will only hurt them later. It's not just the criticisms, but also some of the major doctrines that are seldom taught anymore. What is being neglected (intentionally or not) can become the very thing that causes a crisis of faith later in life. Instead of shying away from difficult topics and questions, we should be embracing them. Intellectual coddling isn't good for anyone.

If we ignore or dodge our questions, we are often allowing doubts to grow. Before souls can be saved, minds must be won. If parents and those in leadership don't prepare students to face the intellectual and spiritual challenges, many will abandon their faith during college or as they start their careers, especially when so many other things are vying for their attention. These are many of the concerns that prompted me to write this book.

Though this book is written primarily for a Christian audience, I've tried to keep in mind those who are curious or skeptical about religion as well. I hope that it will resonate with teenagers and adults alike. If you have questions about faith or are currently having doubts about Christianity in general or the Bible in particular, this book is for you. I have thought about those who believe their view of Christianity is the only version acceptable for entrance into heaven, as well as those who think that everyone might end up there. I've also thought about those who can read the Bible in the original languages and those who have never read it in any language. Much of the content stems from conversations with my two boys and thousands of other students over the years.

It is not a book primarily about Christian doctrine or apologetics, although both emerge from time to time. My intention is not to set myself up as a personal authority but to invite a conversation about difficult topics that are seldom addressed, despite their prevalence in the Bible and history of Christianity. Because topics like hell, the devil, atheism, and prayer are often ridiculed, misunderstood or ignored, Christians need to have thought through these subjects. The main reason why I'm tackling these challenging subjects is because many parents, teachers, and ministers do not, thus leaving a void in one's thinking and ability to respond adequately when the questions and criticisms arise.

Because the Bible is central to one's understanding of Christ and Christianity, the first and longest chapter of the book is devoted to understanding the nature of the Bible, particularly when and how it was formed, common objections, and why it remains so influential. This chapter is intentionally more academic and tries to condense an abundance of foundational information into as few pages as possible.

Fundamentally, everyone believes in something when it comes to religion. Atheists believe there is no god. Atheists are not unreasonable; they are just arguing from a different starting point. The second chapter explores reasons why some people do not to believe in God, what the consequences of disbelief might be, and how an aggressive group of doubters called the "New Atheists" are working tirelessly to rid the world of religion.

Most people know that Jesus is the most influential person in history, yet few people know much about the second most influential (and controversial) figure in history. Despite prevalence in both the Bible and tradition, the devil is rarely a topic of conversation, even among Christians. People often hear sermons about the veracity and authority of the Bible, the importance of faith, family, relationships, and the gospel, yet rarely hear much about what the Bible declares to be the Enemy of them all. Because most people are interested in the supernatural, the third chapter explores the spiritual realm—particularly angels, demons, the differences between bad and evil, and the differences between Hollywood and biblical portrayals of the devil.

Like the devil, the concept of hell has often been shaped more by literature, the arts, and the entertainment industry than what the Bible and tradition have taught. If hell is a real place where a person can spend eternity, this topic also must be taken seriously. The fourth chapter explores the possibility of life beyond the grave, and why reaching a peaceful conclusion about hell should also be a top priority.

Recent national surveys reveal that the majority of people pray, including some with no religious affiliation.[4] Many pray because it makes them feel better, while others think it's a waste of time. Does prayer really work? This chapter explores the nature of prayer, including why and how people pray, and what impact prayer can have on one's life and future.

Just as many teenagers are not ready for what they might face in college, many adults don't know quite what to expect when starting or ending a career. Many people of all ages are uncertain about death and how to make the most of the time they may have left. Therefore, the conclusion explores how precious time is. Each chapter concludes with questions for reflection and suggestions for further

[4] https://www.pewforum.org/religious-landscape-study/frequency-of-prayer/

reading, because my hope is that this book will serve as an accessible, thought-provoking conversation starter for teenagers and adults of all ages. Whether you are heading to college or are well into your career or retirement, this book is for you.

BIBLE MATTERS

Imagine basing your entire life on the content, instruction, and revelation found in a book. This has been the case for Christians for nearly two thousand years. The Bible is the best-selling book in the world year after year. It is the most quoted, referenced, and criticized book as well. The Bible does not need anyone to defend its unique status as being the most influential book in history. It seems that everyone has an opinion of the Bible, even though most people, including Christians, have not read it cover to cover.

A recent national survey revealed that about half of American adults spend time reading the Bible several times per year, and 14 percent on a daily basis.[1] There are many reasons why people don't read the Bible. Some believe that the Bible is boring, too difficult to understand, or that it doesn't seem to resonate with modern culture. Others have no interest in learning more about a warped sense of the Bible that was experienced during their childhood or teenage years. Some refuse to read the Bible because they don't want to discover that certain aspects of their behavior might need to change based on its instruction. Some are too busy, while others are simply too lazy to read the Bible.

---

[1] https://www.barna.com/research/state-of-the-bible-2018-seven-top-findings/

Regardless of your knowledge of the Bible, or lack thereof, I'm sure that you have an opinion of the Bible, just as I do. My guess is that your view of the Bible was shaped by the family, community, or tradition in which you were raised. This is the case for most people. We had several Bibles in our house, including the big one that sat on the coffee table for all to see. We seldom read it as a family, but I believed it to be important. Seeing the words Holy Bible on the cover afforded God's book a special place in our home, and the thought of questioning the divinely inspired, authoritative nature of the Bible never crossed my mind prior to college. I simply believed it to be God's Word because I had never heard otherwise.

It was always comforting to hear people I looked up to share information related to the Bible. I have not forgotten many of the clichés heard along the way: "God will never give us more than we can handle," "the Bible is God's love letter written specifically to you," "meet God in His Word," "the Bible will keep you from sin, or sin will keep you from the Bible," "it is God's road map for your life," and "a dusty Bible will lead to a dirty life."

Many Sunday mornings of my childhood and teenage years were spent listening to Sunday school teachers and preachers convey God's revelation recorded in the Bible. The few times I remember someone asking about how we could know that the Bible really contained the words of Almighty God, preachers and teachers alike would always turn to the Bible to validate and defend its divine nature and relevance for today. Most leaders would point to a couple of verses from the Apostle Paul's second letter written to a young disciple named Timothy:

> All scripture is breathed out by God and profitable for teaching, for reproof, for correction, and for training in righteousness, that the man of God may be competent, and equipped for every good work. (2 Tim. 3:16-17)

That passage always seemed to end the inquiries. Doubting the Bible as being anything other than the very words of God was the last thing on my mind. Though I had not read the entire Bible prior to college, my life had been impacted by what I had heard and read; therefore, when it was time to leave home, I seemed to have an unwavering confidence in its status as the divinely inspired manual for my life. I had no idea that my faith was about to be rocked to the core.

As a student at the University of Texas in Austin, I seized the opportunity to take a class called "The Bible in English and American Literature." It was amazing to think about earning credit for taking a course about the Bible at a massive, secular university. When the professor introduced himself as a former priest, and that the only required book for the course would be the Bible, my excitement grew even more.

However, things took a dramatic turn for the worse when he announced that we would be approaching the Bible as merely one of many great works of literature, and not as the sacred words of God (as I had been taught). When he advised all of the "holy rollers" and "Bible thumpers" to drop the course if offended by his view of scripture, I wrestled with what to do.[2] Rather than drop the course, as half of the other first day attendees had done, I decided to stick it out and be a witness for the Truth.

At one point during the second meeting, the professor asked if anyone wanted to share his or her opinion of the Bible. I was quick to point out the excerpt from Paul's letter to Timothy that I had heard and memorized as the supposed trump card for any Bible doubters.

---

[2] The term *"Bible"* is derived from the word *biblia*, which literally means "the books." Scripture is derived from the Latin word, *scriptura*, meaning "writings." This term refers to the sacred texts that were considered to be inspired by God, accepted by communities of Christ followers, and, therefore, included in the Bible. *Scripture* and *Bible* are synonyms used interchangeably by Christians and throughout this book.

The ensuing questions posed by the professor would forever change my desire to understand the book that Christians over the past two thousand years have read, heard, shared, and followed. After I mentioned the "God-breathed" reference the professor asked if I knew who had written that passage of scripture. I confidently answered, "The Apostle Paul," to which the professor replied, "Someone paid attention in Sunday school." He then asked, "Which particular part of scripture was the Apostle Paul referring to in his letter?" I replied sharply, "*All* scripture." He then asked if I knew when Paul had written the letter, to which I responded, "No."

After the professor explained that the entire New Testament had yet to be written, I realized that Paul was not referring to the entire Bible. The professor then pointed out that Christians should believe that all scripture is "God-breathed," but they should not take that specific passage out of Paul's original context to justify why they believe that all of the Bible is inspired by God. He was right, and I felt stupid, misled, and a little embarrassed. One of the most important lessons I learned was that when Christians quote the Bible out of context, as I did several times during that semester, they can look foolish and encourage skepticism.

When Christians provide inaccurate biblical commentary, as I had done during college, people familiar with the Bible are quick to notice. Imagine if we decided to utilize a great work of literature without actually reading it and then started quoting parts of it out of context and encouraging others to believe our faulty interpretation. How would people who are actually familiar with its content respond to people making such incorrect assertions? This is why so many college students get ripped to shreds when they try to challenge their skeptical professors who have actually read the Bible. Why should a skeptic believe anything related to God or the Bible shared by someone who is ignorant of the scriptures and misuses the little of it that they do know?

Learning from a Skeptic

I'm convinced that my belief in the reliability of the Bible would not have taken shape if not for that college professor who challenged me to know what I believe and back up my beliefs with thoughtful, intelligent responses. Thankfully, unlike many professors who try to discredit and completely undermine the Bible's unique status, my instructor valued my opinion of the Bible. In fact, he was most concerned with my learning the scriptures to form my own conclusions. I'll never forget him saying something like this:

> If you are going to be a Christian, then be a good one. Or if you decide to be an atheist, then be a good one. Just don't believe or assume something to be true just because someone told you it was true along the way. You need to read and discover the truth for yourself. And whatever you do, don't quote stuff out of context when you have no idea what you're talking about. Instead, do your homework, read and study the Bible, ask questions, be willing to go wherever the evidence takes you, and don't be afraid to be wrong or say that you don't know.

Another important thing that I learned from my professor was that most critics are not part of some orchestrated conspiracy to undermine the Bible and turn every Christian into a skeptic or atheist (though some clearly have this agenda). Many critics of the Bible, especially learned college and university professors, have read and studied it for quite some time, and as surprising as it may sound, some have devoted their lives to it. This does not mean that their understanding, interpretation, and criticism of the Bible is correct, but we should not assume that they just need to read the Bible or go to church in order to be convinced of our view of the Bible. Like my professor in college, many of the critics out there are simply trying to have a little fun at the expense of Christians who are ignorant of the Bible that they supposedly hold so dear, yet know so little about. If people are going to hold a high view of scripture, and truly believe it to be the "inspired words of God," then they should know it better than any other book, which also means being familiar with objections to it.

Even though my professor did not believe that the Bible was inspired by God, he taught me things about the Bible that would end up strengthening my faith. It is only fitting that I share some snippets now and expand on them in a moment. For starters, none of the original letters/books (known as autographs) that make up the Bible still exist, for we have only copies of the originals (and these are called manuscripts). This seemed really problematic at first, for if we don't have the original writings, how can we be certain about what they contained?

He also pointed out that there are a few parts of the New Testament that many scholars (including many of the most respected conservative Christian scholars) believe were not part of the original writings based on the discovery and analysis of the oldest surviving ancient manuscripts. The professor explained that Paul, whose letters make up nearly half the New Testament, wrote other letters that did not make it into the Bible, and that Paul himself refers to these "lost" letters in two of his letters that are included in the Bible (1 Cor. 5:9; 2 Cor. 2:4). This made me wonder about why those other letters written by Paul were not included in the New Testament. Were those letters not inspired by God as well?

Furthermore, the professor directed us to passages of scripture that were initially part of the original King James English translation of the Bible published in 1611 that have either become a footnote, placed in brackets, or removed entirely from more modern English translations of the Bible, like the popular New International Version (NIV) or English Standard Version (ESV). We will look at some of these passages in a moment.

He also informed us that Bibles utilized by Catholic Christians contain an extra section of books (known as the Apocrypha) that are placed just between the Old and New Testaments, (or are intermixed with the later portions of the Old Testament). As a Protestant (non-Catholic Christian), this was the first time I had heard of these extra books found in Catholic Bibles. Because of that class, despite my good intentions and years of church and Sunday school attendance, I realized I had very little knowledge of the Bible, and no clue about criticism of the Bible or the process by which the New Testament was written and put together (the canonization process).

As I learned more about criticisms leveled at the Bible, I developed an insatiable desire to read and study it. Though it was difficult at the time, I am very grateful that someone challenged my shallow faith and anemic understanding of the Bible. Dozens of Christians have shared similar stories about times when their faith and understanding of the Bible were challenged by college professors who held a low view of scripture and focused on old arguments as if they were new. The age-old criticisms feel entirely new to credulous, essentially biblically illiterate Christian teenagers, college students, and those new to the Christian faith.

This does not have to be the case, and it is precisely why I have felt compelled to address in this book many of the challenges that I have faced along the way. Despite the criticisms having been around a very long time, there are good, reasonable responses to each objection. Before dealing with the criticisms, however, it is important for one to learn some of the basic aspects of the Bible.

Basics of the Bible

The Bible is bound as a singular book yet consists of a library or collection of sixty-six individual books (such as the book of Nehemiah, the Gospel of Matthew, the Apostle Paul's letter to the Romans, the book of Revelation, etc.). The word *testament* goes back through the Latin word *testamentum* to the Greek word *diatheke*, which typically meant "covenant."[3] Sometimes people refer to the two parts of the Bible as the Old and New "Covenants," but the more common usage has been the Old and New "Testaments." The Hebrew arrangement of the Old Testament books is divided into three sections: the Law (comprised of the first five books of the Bible that is often referred to as the Torah or Pentateuch), the Prophets (arranged into two divisions: "Former Prophets" and "Latter Prophets"), and the Writings (the rest of the Old Testament books).

The Old Testament (Hebrew scriptures) had been recognized as having divine authority and served as a written rule of faith and practice for God's people in the centuries before Jesus walked the earth. The Hebrew Old Testament translated into Greek, referred to as the Septuagint, was heavily used by the authors of the New Testament. Jesus often quoted scripture, and referred to the Old Testament as "the Law, the Prophets, and the Psalms" (Matthew 4:1-10; Luke 24:44), which corresponds to the three-fold division of the Hebrew Bible.[4]

The Old Testament Writing Materials

The time in which the Bible emerged was very different than our

---

[3] Philip Wesley Comfort. *The Origins of the Bible.* (Wheaton, IL: Tyndale, 2003), 5.

[4] The sacred texts that Christians know as the Hebrew Bible or Old Testament is referred to among Jews as the TaNaKh, which is an acronym formed with the first letter of each major section of its threefold division: the Torah (the "Law"), the Nevi'im (the "Prophets"), and the Ketuvim (the "Writings") using the initial Hebrew letters of Torah.

own. Because we live in an age of cameras, the internet, and instantaneous information, it is important to understand the culture that produced and preserved the writings of scripture. All of the books of the Bible were written during an oral culture when writing materials were scarce and most people were illiterate. The Bible mentions that Moses, who lived around 1500 BC, came down from Mount Sinai with two tablets of stone that contained the Ten Commandments (Exod. 31:18; 34:1, 28; Deut. 10:1-5). Though stone seems to be the earliest material used for writing, the Bible mentions that clay tablets were also utilized (Ezra 4:10). Additional materials on which one could write at that time were leather skins (parchment), vellum, and dried up leaves from papyrus plants (papyri would eventually become most commonly used).

Growing up, it never dawned on me that the Bible was actually a collection of dozens of books. The "scriptures" referred to by biblical writers were not yet a Bible bound like we have today, but were a group of scrolls or leaves/pages of papyrus. Prior to the middle of the first century AD, all scriptures and other writings were written on scrolls, typically made of leather parchment or vellum that could be more than thirty feet in length. Parchment was the most durable, and, therefore, most commonly used writing material for the Old Testament. When the Apostle Paul told a disciple named Timothy, "Bring me my parchments," he was referring to scrolls (2 Tim. 4:13). Jesus also read from a scroll when he taught from Isaiah 61 in a synagogue (Luke 4:18).

New Testament Writing Materials

When the New Testament was written during the second half of the first century, the most common writing material used was papyrus. Papyrus plants were plentiful, and oftentimes dried papyri leaves were smoothed out to form a type of paper. Sheets could be glued together to form rolls or scrolls. Eventually the scrolls, which had to be unrolled to be read, were replaced by pages of papyri to form a type of book known as a "codex," similar to our hardback books today. The development of the codex enabled Christian communities to piece together copies of letters, such as the four Gospels, or Paul's writings, to form small booklets that were easier to use than scrolls. By the second half of the second century, codices containing the Gospels were common among Christian communities, and eventually all of the New Testament letters would be bound into one book.

Though papyrus was the most common writing material used, because of exposure to the elements and frequent usage, manuscripts often became brittle and disintegrated within a decade or so. This explains why parchment became the main writing material from about the fourth century through the Middle Ages, and also why we do not have the original New Testament papyri writings. Thankfully, despite the many reasons why the sacred scriptures could have been forgotten, God used a variety of means to preserve what was intended.

Christ and the Gospels

Central to the Christian faith is Jesus Christ, the Word (*logos*) incarnate to which the scriptures bear witness (John 1:1-3). People can know God by knowing Jesus, and learn about Jesus by learning the Bible. Theologian John Frame explains:

> God is very much concerned not only that we believe in Christ, but also that we believe the Word that tells us about Christ, the very Word of God. God has given us not only salvation in Christ, but also a wonderfully simple way to know about that salvation.[5]

[5] John M. Frame. *Apologetics: A Justification of Christian Belief.* Edited by Joseph E. Torres. (Philipsburg, New Jersey: Presbyterian and Reformed Publishing, 2015), 127.

There is no better way to understand who Jesus is than by reading the four Gospels, which are the first four books of the New Testament. Followers of Christ, under divine inspiration, wrote down the significant acts and events of his life and ministry. The New Testament records specific events surrounding Christ's birth, life, ministry, death, and resurrection, as well as the history and development of the early church. Jesus chose twelve disciples (students) to follow him during his three years of formal ministry.[6]

Of the twelve disciples, several wrote letters that became part of the New Testament. Traditionally, Matthew, the tax collector turned Christ follower, wrote the Gospel bearing his name. John wrote five books (the Gospel of John, 1, 2, 3 John, and the book of Revelation), and Peter wrote two letters (1 and 2 Pet.). The four Gospels provide us with biographical sketches of Jesus, and the four respective writers of the Gospels are sometimes referred to as the "Four Evangelists."[7]

Because each of the four Gospel accounts is written by a different person, there are slight variations based on perspective and audience, as well as their aims in recording history.[8] Keep in mind that the Gospels are not exhaustive accounts of everything Jesus said and did, nor do they claim to be. In fact, the Apostle John, stated, "Even the whole world could not contain the books that could be written about the deeds of Jesus" (John 21:25). John was underscoring the fact that his story about Jesus was a selective part of a bigger story, showing a specific purpose for each author. John also explained the main reason

---

[6] We can use the terms *apostle* and *disciple* interchangeably when referring to the Twelve. But there is a distinction. All the apostles were disciples, for it was from a large group of disciples that Jesus designated some to be apostles. This being the case, not all disciples were apostles.

[7] Church tradition has associated each writer with one of the "four living creatures" that are referenced in the Old Testament book of Ezekiel and the New Testament book of Revelation. Matthew has been represented by a man, Mark by a lion, Luke by an ox or calf, and John by an eagle.

[8] See Mark Strauss. *Four Portraits, One Jesus: A Survey of Jesus and the Gospels.* (Grand Rapids: Zondervan, 2007).

for recording what God had revealed:

> That which was from the beginning, which we have heard, which
> we have seen with our eyes, which we have looked at and our hands
> have touched—this we proclaim concerning the Word of life. ...We
> write this to make our joy complete. (1 John 1:1, 4)

The Basic Layout of the New Testament

Most scholars consider the Gospel of Mark, written about AD 65, to be the first biographical account written about Jesus. In addition to the Gospel of Mark, three other biographical sketches written about Jesus (Matthew, Luke, and John) gained widespread acceptance during the first century. Although not the first books to be written in the New Testament, the Gospels were placed at the beginning because they provide biographical information about Jesus Christ, who is the point of the entire Bible. The Gospels of Matthew, Mark, and Luke are referred to as the "Synoptic Gospels" because they include a similar view and rely on similar sources, including each other. The Gospel of John, which was written much later (about AD 90-95), contains a different perspective and is sometimes nicknamed "the theologian's gospel."

The book of Acts is often referred to as the "backbone of the New Testament" because it provides the historical context of the early church and serves as the foundation for the study of the New Testament. Luke, a historian, physician, and traveling missionary companion of the Apostle Paul, wrote both the book of Acts (also known as Acts of the Apostles) and the Gospel of Luke. Luke paid careful attention to detail, and his writings demonstrate a carefully crafted account of events that took place during the earliest days of Christianity. Acts of the Apostles describes Jesus's ascension, the coming of the Holy Spirit at Pentecost, preaching of the gospel by apostles (Peter and John) and other early believers (like Philip), the intensified persecution of the apostles (which God used to spread the gospel), Paul's miraculous conversion from a ruthless Christian persecutor to a Christ follower, his missionary journeys, and much more.

Thirteen of the twenty-seven letters that make up the New Testament are attributed to the Apostle Paul. Paul's letters are arranged primarily based on length (not necessarily when they were written), starting with Romans, which is the longest, and finishing with the shortest letter, Philemon.[9] Some scholars claim that the book of James, written by Jesus's brother between AD 45-49, is the earliest letter in the New Testament, though others believe that either Paul's first letter to the Thessalonians or Galatians may have been written prior. Another of Jesus's brothers, Jude, wrote the New Testament letter that bears his name.[10] Other New Testament books include Hebrews, 1 and 2 Pet., as well as 1, 2, and 3 John. The last book included in the New Testament, the book of Revelation, was written by the Apostle John around AD 95 while he was exiled by Roman authorities on the island of Patmos. The books are typically placed in the following general categories: Gospels, Acts, Paul's (Pauline) Epistles, General Epistles, and Revelation.

Clearly, the New Testament writers felt compelled by the Spirit of God to record what they had seen and heard. Notice the examples:

---

[9] Paul's letters are grouped by those written to churches (Romans to 2 Thessalonians) and those written to individuals (1 Timothy to Philemon). Within each grouping the order is generally longest to shortest.

[10] The New Testament mentions that Jesus had brothers and sisters, and that they did not believe that he was the Messiah until after his resurrection (Mark 6:3, Matt. 13:55-56). Most Protestant Christians believe that the terms *brothers* and *sisters* refer to actual siblings of Jesus. However, because Catholic Christians believe that Mary remained a virgin, most interpret the sibling references as cousins or friends who were very close to family.

- The Apostle John mentions the reason why he wrote his gospel: "that you may believe that Jesus is the Christ, the Son of God, and that by believing you may have life in his name" (John 20:31).

- Luke, addressing a man named Theophilus, explained that he wrote his gospel so "that you may know the certainty of those things in which you were instructed" (Luke 1:4).

- In perhaps the first New Testament letter written, the Apostle Paul stated, this is the "word of God" (1 Thessalonians 2:13). Later in the letter, Paul said, "I command you in the name of the Lord to read this letter to all Christians" (1 Thessalonians 5:27).

- "For no prophecy was ever produced by the will of man, but men spoke from God as they were carried along by the Holy Spirit" (2 Peter 1:21).

- To the church in Corinth, Paul wrote, "What I am writing to you is the Lord's command" (1 Corinthians 14:37).

- The Apostle John said, "Blessed is the one who reads aloud the words of this prophecy, and blessed are those who hear and who keep what is written in it" (Revelation 1:3).

- The Apostle Peter said that Paul's letters are included with "the other scriptures" (2 Peter 3:15-17). Since this was a general letter, widespread knowledge of Paul's authority is thereby implied.

It is clear that all of the New Testament authors believed their respective letters possessed divine authority; however, how did the early believers know whether or not the writings in circulation were worthy of canonization, and thus included in what would become the New Testament? We will now look at the process by which the sacred manuscripts became what we know as the New Testament.

The Canonization of the New Testament

The word *canon* (borrowed from the Greek *kanon*) means a rule or standard for measurement.[11] With respect to the Bible, it speaks of those books that met a specific standard and, therefore, were worthy of inclusion in the canon of the scriptures. Since the fourth century, the word *canon* has been used by Christians to denote a list of authoritative books belonging to the Old and New Testaments.

The Old Testament was written over a period of about 1500 years, whereas the twenty-seven separate writings (referred to as books or letters) that make up the New Testament were written during the second half of the first century (which is within a single generation). The New Testament books were written in a particular language (Koine Greek), during a particular period of time (between roughly AD 45-95), in a particular geographical, historical, and cultural setting (Palestine and Greco-Roman) by particular people (apostles and their associates), for particular needs of specific individuals and groups of people (communities of believers—the Church).

Christians acknowledge that God is the ultimate author of the Bible even though humans were involved in the process. The books were written by men who were inspired by the Spirit of God to preserve and transmit what had been conveyed orally by the apostles, eyewitnesses, and the earliest Christians.[12] Therefore, each book contains both human and divine aspects. Naturally, the personality and writing style and aims of the authors are present within the scriptures even though the supernatural Spirit of God inspired what was written. All of this may seem difficult to fathom at the moment, but there is one thing I want

---

[11] *Kanon* is the Greek rendering of an even older semitic word *qaneh*, which means stick or reed.

[12] This would refer to the Gospels specifically, and Acts (at least to some extent since Luke would have had Paul's and his own experiences recorded in the book). The epistles and Revelation were written documents from the start.

to make very clear—because of the providential guidance of God, we can be confident in the accuracy, authority, and dependability of the Bible we now possess. Because the Lord was directly involved in the composition, compilation, and preservation of the books that make up the Bible, it is completely trustworthy, reliable, and authoritative.

It is important to note that the Bible was considered authoritative long before it was canonized. In other words, God had inspired communities through the apostles' teaching before the words were written down and circulated among communities of believers (the Church). God spoke through human authors to teach people what to believe and how to live, and then communities of Christians preserved the original teachings through oral communication and later through writing down and circulating the divinely inspired words.

The canonization "process" of the New Testament lasted for nearly 300 years, as synods (councils) of leaders met to affirm and reaffirm what the Christian communities had heard, believed, taught, recorded in writing, and, at times, even died to uphold. All of the church Councils were significant, but two stand out regarding the canonization process of the New Testament—the Synod of Hippo in AD 393 and the Council of Carthage in AD 397. During these councils, church leaders affirmed a list of twenty-seven books that had been previously mentioned in a letter written by a bishop from Alexandria named Athanasius in AD 367. The twenty-seven letters first mentioned by Athanasius and reaffirmed at the Councils of Hippo and Carthage are the precise writings that make up the New Testament we possess today. The church leaders at these councils did not confer upon the twenty-seven books any authority that they did not already possess, but simply attested their previously established canonicity.[13]

---

[13] F.F. Bruce. *The Books and Parchments: How We Got Our English Bible.* (Basingstoke: Pickering and Inglis, 1984), 13.

How Decisions Were Made

Though it may come as a surprise to some Christians, the New Testament, in its full and complete form of twenty-seven books, did not just supernaturally appear one day many centuries ago. As previously mentioned, the canonization process was a long (and sometimes complicated) historical development that lasted nearly three hundred years, and human beings played a role in that development.[14] One of the most common questions pertaining to the canon of the New Testament is, "How were the canonical books distinguished from the non-canonical books?" The short answer is that the canon was determined by the response from the community of Christ followers. Each letter in circulation had to reveal apostolic authorship or endorsement, receive widespread support from Christian communities, and mirror the teachings of Christ and the apostles. Each book/letter had to meet the following standards:

Apostolic Endorsement - the work was either written by an apostle (like the writings of Paul or John) or endorsed by an apostle. Mark and Luke were not apostles, but Matthew and John were. Luke was a companion who traveled with Paul and wrote the gospel of Luke and the book of Acts. Paul *endorsed* Luke's writings, and the Gospel of Mark was endorsed by Peter.

Widespread Acceptance - If there was a question, then a debate would ensue, and the evidence would be examined. The author of the book of Hebrews was a master writer, seemingly very intelligent based on literary style, yet nobody knows for sure who wrote it. For many years it was believed that the Apostle Paul wrote the book of Hebrews, but this is not the consensus among scholars today. It was included in the New Testament canon because the church accepted it as being divinely inspired and in agreement with what they had witnessed and believed.

---

[14] Michael J. Kruger. *Canon Revisited: Establishing the Origins and Authority of the New Testament Books.* (Wheaton, IL: Crossway, 2012), 34.

Every book had to gain widespread acceptance, even though each started with local recognition. There were times when communities of Christians debated and changed their minds about certain letters in circulation, but the central core of the New Testament books was considered authoritative early on in the canonization process. By the middle of the first century, the words of Jesus, which were considered just as authoritative as the Hebrew scriptures, were being written by people who witnessed his death and resurrection.

The process of canonization was not about the church making anything official as much as it was about the church acknowledging the divinely inspired apostolic teachings and writings that had been accepted by communities of believers. Therefore, much of what was officially approved by the Councils as scripture was merely a "rubber stamp" on what books were unofficially accepted as divinely inspired by the believing communities.

Apostolic Teaching – What mattered most was what the letter/book taught about the person and work of Christ, thus mirroring the tradition of apostolic teachings. If a particular writing maintained the testimony of the apostolic witness to Jesus's crucifixion and resurrection, then inclusion was a possibility. Some letters in circulation claimed similar authority to the letters that eventually would make up the canonical New Testament. Because all of the New Testament writings had not been collected as one "book" until the later part of the second century, some communities accepted a few letters that would not be included in the canon, such as *The Shepherd of Hermas* and *Letter to Barnabas*.

Paul's Other Letters

The Apostle Paul, who wrote nearly half of the New Testament letters, mentions having written other letters that are not included in the New Testament canon (1 Cor. 5:9, Col. 4:16). Naturally, one may ask, "Why were some of Paul's letters not included in the New Testament canon?" The simple answer is that they were not intended to be part of the canon, just as some of what Jesus said and did was not included in the Bible (John 20:30). It does not mean that certain events did not occur, or that Paul's other letters were not orthodox. But since no copies of Paul's "other" letters exist, there is no point in speculating about their inclusion or exclusion.

The Old Testament Apocrypha

It was confusing to hear for the first time during my college class that not all Bibles contained the same number of books. Given that we were talking about the Bible, once again, I felt like I had been misled by childhood teachers who probably did not know what I was learning. After doing a little homework, I realized that there are two common questions raised when people discover that not all Bibles contain the same number of books: First, why are certain books that were originally included in the canon no longer present in most Bibles, particularly the Apocrypha that was included in the original King James English version published in 1611? Second, why do Bibles used by Catholic and Orthodox Christians still contain the Apocrypha?

Catholic Christians prefer the term *deuterocanonical*, derived from the word *deuteros*, meaning "second," because the books of the Apocrypha were not part of the earliest canon but accepted later as a second canon. The fourteen to fifteen books that make up the Apocrypha (depending on how they are organized) were written during a five-hundred-year period (roughly 400 BC to AD 100) and typically included in a separate section that followed, or were intermixed with, the Old Testament in Bibles produced before the sixteenth-century Reformation. The Apocrypha books are as follows:

1. The First Book of Esdras (also known as Third Esdras)
2. The Second Book of Esdras (also known as Fourth Esdras)

3. Tobit

4. Judith

5. The Additions to the Book of Esther

6. The Wisdom of Solomon

7. Ecclesiasticus, or the Wisdom of Jesus the Son of Sirach

8. Baruch

9. The Letter of Jeremiah (this letter is sometimes incorporated as the last chapter of Baruch; When this is done, the number of books is fourteen instead of fifteen)

10. The Prayer of Azariah and the Song of the Three Young Men

11. Susanna

12. Bel and the Dragon

13. The Prayer of Manasseh

14. The First Book of Maccabees

15. The Second Book of Maccabees[15]

The Gnostic Writings

Though the Apocrypha was included with the Old Testament, some additional manuscripts emerged during the second and third centuries that were not accepted by the early church. Most of these "apocryphal" writings (not to be mistaken with the Old Testament Apocrypha) began circulating among Christian communities and came to be known as the "Gnostic writings" because some claimed that secret or hidden knowledge (*gnosis* in Greek) was needed to understand the scriptures. Historian Jeffery Bingham explains:

---

[15] This chart and a concise explanation of the arrangement of the Old Testament Apocrypha are explained by Neil Lightfoot in *How We Got the Bible*, 164-166. At the Council of Trent, held in 1546, the Roman Catholic Church pronounced the Old Testament Apocrypha (except 1 and 2 Esdras, and the Prayer of Manasseh) as canonical Scripture. Because Protestant Christians do not believe the Apocrypha is inspired by God, it is absent from their Bibles.

The Gnostic writings were dualistic in nature, claiming that the Spirit is good, but the body and other physical things are bad; the Spirit Christ is the true Savior, but the human Jesus is only a shell; the New Testament is the good news of salvation, but the Old Testament is a record of false teaching.[16]

Many of these writings contained historical inaccuracies and stories about Jesus and the apostles that are rather bizarre and in no way meet the criteria of canonization that was explained earlier. The majority of Gnostic writings were rejected not only because of divergent theology, but also because they were written a century or more later than the New Testament writings. Clearly these writings did not pass the canonicity test of receiving apostolic endorsement, bearing an apostolic witness, and being accepted by the Christian communities. Though Gnosticism may have been the most widespread of the second-century heretical groups, it did not last very long. Despite a few of the apocryphal or extra-biblical New Testament letters gaining acceptance within some of the earliest Christian communities, particularly *The Gospel of Thomas* and *The Shepherd of Hermas*, none of them were considered for canonical status at any of the major councils.

New Testament Writers' Knowledge of the Extra-biblical Sources

It is interesting to note that several New Testament writers appear to have knowledge of extra-biblical sources. Jude, the Lord's brother, whose New Testament letter bears his name, makes reference to extra-biblical writings, including the *Assumption of Moses*, and *1 Enoch* (vv. 14-15). The Apostle Paul also utilized extra-biblical resources in order to meet his audience on their terms, thus demonstrating that

---

[16] D. Jeffrey Bingham. *Pocket History of the Church*. (Downers Grove, IL: InterVarsity, 2002), 40.

all truth is God's truth, even if it is not "canonical" (Acts 17:16-34, 2 Tim. 3:8; Titus 1:12). James, in his New Testament epistle, also makes several allusions to the wisdom found in non-biblical literature prevalent at the time.[17]

Such references reveal the importance of being familiar with the culture in which one lives, as well as the importance of conveying truth in ways that are relatable and relevant. Yet, it does not mean that the biblical authors' use of such references signify that these extra-biblical works were authoritative in the same sense, but that they could be utilized to articulate truth.

The Canonical Heritage of the Church

Before the New Testament canon was acknowledged and utilized, the Holy Spirit worked within the church and ancient creeds. The word *creed*, which comes from the Latin word *credo*, means "I believe." The faith of the earliest Christians was developed by the scriptures they possessed, and through the traditions and practices of the early church, especially the creeds. This is news to most Protestant Christians who are unfamiliar with the sacraments and traditions of the church.[18] Historian Ted Campbell points out that, "Catholic and Eastern Orthodox traditions have insisted on the interconnected nature of the scriptures and other traditions handed down from Christ and the early church, which is something that many Protestants have yet to realize."[19]

An enormous debt is owed to the early church, and many subse-

---

[17] There are many parallels between the Book of Sirach that was popular among wisdom literature during the first century and the New Testament letter written by James.

[18] William J. Abraham. *Crossing the Threshold of Divine Revelation*. (Grand Rapids, MI: Eerdmans, 2006), 100.

[19] Ted A. Campbell. *Christian Mysteries*. (Eugene, OR: Wipf & Stock, 2005), 18.

quent generations of believers, whom God used to form and preserve the creeds, scriptures and sacraments. New Testament scholar N.T. Wright suggests that Christians should let tradition and scripture flow together straightforwardly into a single stream.[20] Scripture is the surest guide to help us understand who God is and where we should be going as disciples of Christ. But traditions help us to know where we have come from and how the Holy Spirit worked in and through the lives of previous generations of saints, not to mention how the Lord is still nourishing souls today.

Without church Councils we would not have the Bible as it exists today, for the Lord used previous generations of Christian leaders to affirm the scriptures and defend against false teaching. Extra-biblical traditions and practices (e.g., the Apostles' Creed, the Nicene Creed, and doctrine of the Trinity found therein), though not on par with scripture, should be revered and embraced along with the Bible as being vital parts of the canonical heritage of the church.

Not only do creeds affirm and explain scripture, but they have often been used to summarize belief about God. Creeds have also been utilized to explain the gospel. The shortest creed, "Jesus Christ is Lord," is cited throughout Paul's letters (1 Cor. 12:3; Phil. 2:11). Creeds have often been used by groups of Christians in spiritual formation and worship. Embracing these extra-biblical traditions can only aid Christians in their spiritual development, witness, and defense of the Faith. Because many Christians do not have an adequate understanding of the Trinitarian faith of the church, utilization of the Apostles' Creed and Nicene Creed can also help strengthen one's understanding of the doctrine of the Trinity.

If someone were to ask a Christian about his or her religious be-

[20] N.T. Wright. *Scripture and the Authority of God: How To Read The Bible Today.* (New York: Harper One, 2012), 120.

liefs, responding with the Apostles' Creed would be a great answer. In addition to scripture and creeds, the canonical heritage of the church includes baptism, the Eucharist, singing, memorization of doctrinal summaries, and the like. All have been used as effective means of grace, with the guidance of the Holy Spirit, to help sinners become more like Christ. Embracing the "expanded canon" as a means of grace, though not to be perceived as primary or superior to scripture, can serve to strengthen one's faith and witness.

A Brief Timeline of the New Testament Canonization & Publication

Christian leaders during the first few centuries of Christianity (sometimes referred to as "church fathers"), such as Ignatius (ca. 107), Polycarp (ca. 155), Justin Martyr (ca. 165), Irenaeus (ca. 180) and Clement (ca. 198) used the bulk of the material contained in the New Testament within their writings.

Papias, Bishop of Hierapolis (ca. 130-140), in a work preserved for us by the historian Eusebius (ca. 339), mentioned the names of the Gospel writers Matthew and Mark, thus indicating his acceptance of them as canonical.

The second-century Gnostic writer Marcion produced a limited canon of his own (ca. 140), rejecting the entire Old Testament and settling only for a portion of the New Testament—Luke's Gospel (eliminating chapters 1 and 2), and ten of Paul's letters. He also accepted Ephesians, though he substituted the name "Laodiceans." Many scholars believe that Marcion's heretical canon caused some orthodox Christians to establish a New Testament canon.

Tatian (ca. 160), a pupil of Justin Martyr, in the *Diatessaron*, mentioned that four Gospels had been accepted by the church.

170 - *The Muratorian Canon* was discovered and published in 1740 by a librarian named L.A. Muratori. Many scholars date the origin of the fragment between the second and fourth centuries. It provides the oldest canon

list, referencing twenty-two of the twenty-seven books that make up the New Testament as we see it today.

Irenaeus of Lyons (ca. 180), who was a student of Polycarp, first used the term *New Testament* and also provided the order of the four Gospels that are included in the New Testament. In addition, Irenaeus referenced Acts, 1 Peter, 1 John, and all of Paul's letters except Philemon, and the book of Revelation.

Tertullian (ca. 225), a North African church father in the early third century, was one of the first (along with Irenaeus) to call the scriptures the "New Testament," placing it on a level of inspiration and authority with the Old Testament.

Origen (ca. 254), a prodigious scholar, made critical studies of the New Testament text and also wrote commentaries and sermons on most books of the New Testament, emphasizing their inspiration by God.

303-306 - Emperor Diocletian's persecution included confiscating and destroying New Testament Scriptures.

Eusebius (ca. 339), bishop of Caesarea, a great church historian, set forth his estimate of the canon in his *Church History*. Eusebius considered the following books canonical: the four Gospels, Acts, Paul's letters, 1 Peter, 1 John, and Revelation. He also mentioned that James, 2 Peter, 2 and 3 John, and Jude were contested books.

In 367, Athanasius, bishop of Alexandria, in his *Festal Letter* for Easter, provided the earliest document that specified the twenty-seven books we have in the New Testament today.

In 397, the Council of Carthage reaffirmed the twenty-seven books mentioned by Athanasius three decades earlier. At this point the books of the Bible were officially agreed upon.

Around 405, Jerome, a monk, brilliant scholar, and the most learned man of his age, translated the Bible into Latin (called the *Vulgate*, after the Latin term, which means "common"). The Vulgate contained all twenty-seven books of the New Testament. Some, including Jerome's contemporary, Augustine of Hippo, were not enthusiastic about Jerome's translation because he chose to translate directly from the Hebrew instead of translating from the Greek text of the Jewish scriptures (Septuagint). Jerome's Vulgate would serve as the Bible of choice for the next one thousand years.

1200s - Stephen Langton, a lecturer at the University of Paris, created chapter divisions in the Bible.

1382 - John Wycliff, an Oxford scholar and priest, translated Jerome's Latin Bible (the Vulgate) into English.

1455 - The Gutenberg Printing Press was invented in Germany. The Vulgate was the very first book printed.

1516 - Erasmus of Rotterdam was the first to publish the printed Greek New Testament from his own Latin translation and some Greek manuscripts. He was one of Europe's leading scholars who knew the original languages of the Bible.

1525 - William Tyndale, an Oxford scholar, translated the New Testament into English from the original Greek text.

1534 - Martin Luther translated the Bible into German, utilizing much of Erasmus's Greek New Testament.

1536 - Tyndale's outspokenness, coupled with King Henry VIII's opposition to his translation of the New Testament into English a decade earlier, resulted in a death sentence for Tyndale. Tyndale was captured by the king's soldiers, strangled, and burned alive. His last words would turn out to be prophetic. As the fire was being lit, Tyndale said, "Lord, open the king of England's eyes." Within just a few years, the king would authorize Tyndale's translation of the Bible, which is why he has been referred to as the "Father of the English Bible."

1537 - Matthew's Bible was published, which was a compilation of the work of William Tyndale and a friend named John Rogers. Because Rogers published it under the pseudonym "Thomas Matthew," it became known as the Matthew Bible or Matthew's Bible.

1539 - The Great Bible was published, which was a revision of Matthew's Bible. Another friend of Tyndale, Miles Coverdale, edited the new edition that would become the first authorized English Bible to be read in churches. King Henry placed a Bible in every English church. Being able to read the Bible in their own language created quite a stir among the laity. So much so, that in order to prevent theft, Bibles were chained to the pillars of the church.

1551 - Robert Estienne (who preferred the Latin name Stephanus) divided the text of the Bible into verses.

1555 - England's Catholic Queen Mary Tudor outlawed all English Bible versions and persecuted Protestants.

1560 - A new English translation was produced in Switzerland called the Geneva Bible. It was the first to include both chapters and verses. The Geneva Bible was used by Shakespeare and was also brought to Plymouth on the Mayflower.

1611 - King James I of England commissioned around fifty Hebrew and Greek scholars to translate the Bible from twenty-five available Hebrew and Greek manuscripts that were produced in the twelfth and thirteenth centuries. After roughly about four years, the King James Version Bible became very popular in public worship and private usage. It contained the Apocrypha books that are excluded from Protestant Bibles today.

1952 - The Revised Standard Version (RSV) was published. It would undergo several revisions in subsequent decades.

1971 - The New American Standard Bible (NASB) was published.

1978 - The New International Version (NIV) was published. It became the Bible translation of choice for most evangelical Christians for the next few decades.

2001 - The English Standard Bible (ESV) was published. It has become another widely embraced Bible translation among evangelical Christians.

The discovery of more ancient biblical manuscripts, as well as the development of certain languages (i.e., Old English to modern English), both led to updated translations of the Bible. One must realize that modern translations of the Bible are not removing words; they are translating from thousands of Greek texts that are dated prior to the fourteenth-century copies that were used to translate the King James English translation of the Bible in the early 1600s. New Testament scholar Craig Blomberg correctly points out that modern translations are actually "restoring the original text."[21] This is why studying multiple translations enables one to notice the differences and value of translations, and better understand the process through which God inspired, communicated, and preserved sacred scripture. [22]

Textual Criticism

Now that we have covered some basics about the content and preservation of the Bible, let's move on to the subject of textual criticism, which is the basis for many of the challenges that students encounter during college and later in life. Textual criticism is the science of studying ancient manuscripts to determine what the original text stated at the time of its transmission. In relation to the Bible, the traditional purpose of textual criticism was ideally to recover the original text (autograph) of the New Testament from the available manuscript evidence. Leading New Testament scholar

[21] Craig L. Blomberg. *Can We Still Believe The Bible: An Evangelical Engagement With Contemporary Questions.* (Grand Rapids, MI: Brazos Press, 2014), 37-39.
[22] Neil R. Lightfoot. *How We Got the Bible.* (Grand Rapids: Baker Books, 2003). I am indebted to the wisdom, scholarship, and history contained in this outstanding resource, much of which is summarized within the timeline provided in this chapter. I am also grateful to the late Howard Hendricks of Dallas Seminary for teaching me the importance of studying numerous translations of the Bible.

Bruce Metzger stated that "the textual critic seeks to ascertain from divergent copies which form of the text should be regarded as most nearly conforming to the original."[23] This type of study was confined mostly to those in the academy (colleges, universities, and seminaries) for decades, and the main goal was always to establish as best as possible what the original authors/writers wrote.

The task of the textual critic is to take the copies of the original manuscripts, carefully analyze them, and then determine the best estimation of what was originally written. We have 600 copies of Homer's writings, but the closest to the original is 500 years after the events occurred. There are only seven copies of Plato's manuscripts, and those documents are dated around 1,200 years after the originals. For most ancient works other than the New Testament there are only an average of 10 to 20 copies with which to compare.

The reliability and abundance of New Testament manuscripts in comparison to all other ancient documents that have been discovered is staggering. The total number of copies of Greek New Testament manuscripts that have been found is approaching 5,800 (whether in fragments or collections), and sometimes in the hundreds per book of the New Testament. Additionally, there are nearly 10,000 Latin manuscripts, plus another 8,000 manuscripts in Ethiopic, Slavic, and Armenian that have been discovered.[24]

What makes the unprecedented number of New Testament manuscripts even more remarkable is how many copies agree with each other, especially ones that have emerged from different geographical areas and sometimes written in different languages. This demonstrates that the stories that had been first transmitted orally, and later

---

[23] Bruce M. Metzger. *The Text of the New Testament: Its Transmission, Corruption, and Restoration*, 2nd edition. (New York: Oxford University Press, 1968), xv.

[24] Lee Strobel. *The Case for Christ*. (Grand Rapids: Zondervan, 1998), 63.

preserved in written form, occurred with accuracy and integrity. In comparison to other ancient documents, it is easy to conclude that the attestation for the reliability of the New Testament documents is far and away the most accurate and reliable of any ancient document in history.[25]

As more manuscripts have been found, the picture has become even clearer, for the vast majority of discovered manuscripts contain essentially the same information, regardless of the age of the manuscript or location in which it was found. Furthermore, numerous citations in the writings of the early church fathers also serve as a primary source in validating the New Testament. It has been said that if all of the New Testament manuscripts were destroyed, the text of the New Testament could still be restored from the quotations made by the church fathers.[26] Based on the evidence, Christians should be fully confident about the veracity of scripture. Because of the providential guidance of God, we can trust the accuracy, authority, and dependability of the Bible we now possess.

Variations

Despite the existence of thousands of ancient manuscripts that have preserved the heart of what the original autographs contained, some non-Christian textual critics from the mid-nineteenth century onward have chosen to focus mostly on minor variants (a misspelled word, omission or insertion of a word, or changes in word order in the text).

[25] The earliest manuscript we have is of the Gospel of John, referred to as P52. It is dated between AD 110-125, which is about eighty to ninety years after the crucifixion and events it records, and only within twenty-five years of the traditional date of the original Gospel of John. Most of the earliest manuscripts we have are dated during the late second century, which is about 100 years after the autographs). These New Testament manuscripts are dated much earlier than many of the manuscripts we have of other ancient documents.

[26] David Alan Black. *New Testament Textual Criticism: A Concise Guide.* (Grand Rapids, MI: Baker Books, 1994), 24.

This newer and more prevalent form of textual criticism is common in college religious studies courses taught by skeptics across the country. In addition to pointing out grammatical or spelling errors, some critics become fixated on what appears to be alterations, corruption, or contradictions of the original texts. Ironically, any scholar making such claims is essentially admitting that one can know the intentions of the biblical writers and what the original writings said.[27]

Textual criticism is no longer confined to college campuses in large part due to the emergence of the internet and several best-selling books. Bart Erhman's *New York Times* best-seller, *Misquoting Jesus*, introduced thousands in the general populace to this more modern, skeptical form of textual criticism that has dominated religious and New Testament studies departments in the academy for decades. Despite the growth and prevalence of this approach to textual criticism among the general populace, it is important to acknowledge that some critics are not trying to undermine the authority and reliability of the Bible.

In fact, there are many things that Christians can learn from textual critics and skeptical professors, even those who are not Christians. Ehrman correctly points out that, "Most readers, even those interested in Christianity, the Bible and biblical studies, both those who believe the Bible is inerrant and those who do not, know nothing about textual criticism."[28] Ehrman is exactly right, and those who do not learn about textual criticism and other issues skeptics are posing are likely to be misled or discouraged by such teaching. It is also important to realize that there are many resources available that explain, and oftentimes refute, the arguments being made by textual critics.[29]

---

[27] See Andreas J. Kostenberger, Darrell L. Bock and Josh D. Chatraw. *Truth in a Culture of Doubt: Engaging Skeptical Challenges to the Bible.* (Nashville: B&H Publishing, 2014), 79-106.

[28] Bart D. Ehrman. *Misquoting Jesus: The Story Behind Who Changed The Bible and Why.* (New York: Harper Collins, 2005), 15.

[29] See the "For Further Reading" section at the end of this chapter. .

Obviously, many of the thousands of copies of the New Testament manuscripts contain differences (variants), and with each new discovery of an ancient manuscript there will be more variants identified. Aware of this, some textual critics propose an exaggerated number of variants or discrepancies between the textual manuscripts in order to cast doubt on the divinely inspired, authoritative nature of the Bible. This is often the first thing pointed out by critics, even though they are well aware that the vast majority of variants are very minor and inconsequential. Some skeptics claim that there are nearly four hundred thousand textual variants among the ancient New Testament manuscripts.[30] The high number of variants results from dealing with thousands upon thousands of manuscripts. As more ancient manuscripts are discovered, the number of variants will increase. Though some critics will continue to focus on elevated numbers of variants, nothing changes in terms of the reliability of the New Testament. Leading New Testament scholar Craig Blomberg explains:

> Less than 3 percent of variants are significant enough to be presented in two standard critical editions of the Greek New Testament, and only about a tenth of 1 percent are interesting enough to make their way into footnotes in most English translations.[31]

Because of the abundance of New Testament manuscripts that agree, it has been fairly easy for scholars to identify ones that do not. Though scribes were meticulous in copying the scriptures, there were rare occasions when one might insert a word or phrase with the intention of clarifying or explaining a particular verse or passage of scripture (as seen with John 5:4, which we will look at in a moment).

[30] Bart D. Ehrman. *Jesus, Interrupted: Revealing The Hidden Contradictions in the Bible (and Why We Don't Know About Them).* (New York: Harper Collins, 2009), 16-17.

[31] Craig L. Blomberg. *Can We Still Believe The Bible?*, 27.

Despite these rare insertions, anyone who is curious or even skeptical about the validity of the Bible should realize that the majority of biblical scholars claim that the New Testament, which has been reconstructed using copies of the original ancient manuscripts, is more than 99.5 percent identical to the original writings that no longer exist.[32] The critics who claim that there are major discrepancies in the New Testament are focusing on 0.5 percent of the text, which is an extremely small percentage. By taking criticism seriously, Christians can become even more confident in the reliability of the New Testament.

By understanding textual criticism, one can easily see that the "contradictions" and "variants" brought up by skeptics are usually the result of different biblical authors describing the same events or an inadvertent misspelling or omission made by a copyist. Understanding textual criticism also enables one to realize that the insertions made by copyists do not negate, contradict, or undermine anything that happened. If Christians are not taught about what skeptical books and teachers are proposing, many will continue to be misled. This is all the more reason why people (especially teenagers and college students) need to be aware not only of the basics of textual criticism, but also blind spots inherent within some Christian circles.

Problematic Passages in the Bible?

I remember being frustrated the first time I heard a college

---

[32] Archibald T. Robertson. *An Introduction to Textual Criticism of the New Testament.* (Nashville, TN: Broadman, 1925), 22. Lee Strobel. *The Case for Christ.* (Grand Rapids: Zondervan, 1998), 260. An argument has been put forward that the trustworthiness of the copy and transmission process is evident in what we can observe among existing manuscripts. However, there is a wing of scholarship (Ehrman among them, of course) who would say we don't have any way to know how much even our earliest manuscripts might differ from the originals because there is a gap between the originals and the earliest copies.

professor claim that some passages should not be included in the Bible. The reason why many Christians are not familiar with the disputed passages pointed out by scholars is because they either have not read the Bible or failed to notice the notations in their Bible. I invite you to open a Bible to learn about the passages that some scholars question whether or not they should be included in the Bible:

John 5:4 –The Missing Verse

To provide a glimpse of a common exercise that some professors conduct in class, please open a Bible and turn to the Gospel of John chapter 5. Starting with verse 1, read through verse 5. Did you notice anything odd about verse 4 in your Bible? If you are reading the New International Version (NIV) or English Standard Version (ESV), verse 4 is missing entirely! The numbering of the verses jumps from verse 3 to verse 5. The editors of these popular translations chose to completely remove verse 4. Why? What did it say? Is there a notation in your Bible? Maybe not, but you can turn to the King James Version (KJV) translation of the Bible that was first published in 1611 or the New American Standard Bible (NASB) and read the missing fourth verse that has been removed from most modern English translations. The verse in question read:

> For an angel of the Lord went down at certain seasons into
> the pool and stirred up the water; whoever then first, after the
> stirring up of the water, stepped in was made well from whatever
> disease with which he was afflicted. (John 5:4 NASB)

After reading this seemingly odd verse that was not in my Bible, I could not wait to discover what some respected theologians and pastors have said about it. Several ministers mentioned to me that they were unaware of the "missing" verse. One claimed that the Bible editors must have made a mistake. My next step of inquiry was to look at a trusted commentary on the Gospel of John. Since commentators are typically experts who have devoted many years to studying particular books in the Bible, certainly I could find out about this missing verse in a commentary, right?

To my surprise, all of the commentators mentioned that this verse should not be included in the New Testament Gospel of John because it does not exist in the earliest, most reliable manuscripts that have been discovered in recent years. It was originally contained in the King James English translation of the Bible that was based on two dozen manuscripts dating from the twelfth and thirteenth centuries, but since the majority of older manuscripts (by "older," we mean closer to the first-century New Testament time period in which the original letter was written) do not contain this verse, even the most respected Christian biblical scholars believe that it should not be included in the Bible.

It was likely added by a later scribe to help readers understand the significance of getting in the water when it was stirred (because that is the reason the lame man gave for his ongoing illness; when the waters were stirred others got in before him). Most English translations of the Bible either contain a footnote or place this verse in brackets. This is a classic example of a variant that does not shape or change any significant doctrine or diminish the Bible's witness.

Mark 16:9-20 The Longer Ending of Mark

Now let us take a look at the ending of the Gospel of Mark, specifically chapter 16, verses 9 through 20. Unlike the fourth verse of the fifth chapter of the Gospel of John that was either erased or banished to the footnote section in the NIV, ESV, and many other English translations of the New Testament, you will notice the following disclaimer listed after verse 8 in the sixteenth chapter of Mark's

Gospel: [Some of the earliest manuscripts do not include 16:9-20].
Just like the missing verse in the Gospel of John, most commentators,
even conservative evangelical ones, treat this passage with suspicion
and claim that it should not be considered part of the New Testament
because the vast majority of the oldest and most reliable manuscripts
do not contain these verses.

Further, it does not seem to fit the context of the rest of the
chapter. Just read those last eleven verses of Mark's Gospel and you
will notice that it seems rather out of place. This passage has caused a
lot of confusion, not to mention being neglected by most Christians.
After all, who wants to drink poison or handle venomous snakes out of
obedience to God that will serve as a sign of their salvation? Leading
New Testament scholar F.F. Bruce stated, "the longer part of Mark's
Gospel was not part of Mark's work, and clearly the content of the
passage reveals its secondary nature."[33] There are numerous reasons
given by scholars about why the longer ending to Mark's Gospel and
the missing verse from the fifth chapter of John's Gospel should not
be included in the Bible:

1. Scribes chose to add verses 9-20 because it would seem
    odd for Mark to end verse eight in an abrupt fashion
    without mentioning anything about the risen Lord ap-
    pearing to anyone.

2. The content of this passage seems very strange and there-
    fore does not fit with the rest of the chapter or Mark's
    Gospel. So why would a scribe mention something as
    odd as people handling snakes and not being harmed
    as a sign of being a Christian? Most scholars claim that
    the scribes who added these verses were thinking of the

---

[33] F.F. Bruce. *The Canon of Scripture.* (Downers Grove, IL: InterVarsity, 1988), 288.

Apostle Paul's miraculous experience of having been bitten by a poisonous snake and feeling no ill effects (recorded in Acts 28:3-6) or Jesus mentioning that his disciples would tread on snakes without ill effect (Luke 10:19).

3. Other scholars point out that the style of writing in the Greek differs significantly from the style of writing in the rest of Mark's Gospel, and therefore could not have been part of the original text.

In addition to the reasons given as to why scholars believe these verses should not be included in the New Testament, one may ask if the events may have really happened or not, and, if so, why should they not be included in the canon? For an explanation, see the previous section about the canonization of the New Testament. In terms of dealing with the issue at hand, one must keep in mind that the goal of textual criticism is not to determine whether what is found in a manuscript is true or not, but whether or not it was originally part of the original writing (autograph) as constructed, based on the most reliable surviving manuscripts.

A few other "problematic" passages pointed out by critics are John 7:53-8:11 (the story of the woman caught in adultery), 1 John 5:7, and Matthew 6:13. All of the aforementioned passages are not found in the earliest manuscripts, and all biblical scholars are aware of it. It is the reason why most Bibles make notations of these additions. It does not necessarily mean that the events did not occur; it just means that they were not included in the original manuscripts of the New Testament.

How Should One Respond to Legitimate Criticism of the Bible?

When Christians hear for the first time that many scholars suggest a verse or passage of scripture should not be included in the

Bible, confusion, disbelief, or resentment typically follows. Some believe that critics are involved in a conspiracy or concerted effort to undermine the authority of the Bible. This is usually not the case. In response to the apparent contradictions, missing verses, variants, and valid questions posed by critics, Christians sometimes attempt either to prove too much, or fail to respond at all. I have heard ministers respond by saying, "You have to have faith" or "Let's pray that God will open the eyes of these blind people." I remember one minister instructing his audience "just to trust God to deal with the critics who are persecuting you because Jesus was persecuted and predicted that you will be as well."

All the while, an intellectually honest approach to the interpretation of scripture is ignored, and well-meaning Christians continue to fit the caricatures of their critics. In addition to witnessing college students struggle with these issues, I've known seminary graduates who abandoned their trust in the reliability of the Bible when their childhood view was challenged.

Some evangelical pastors along the way have not shied away from bringing up important issues of textual criticism with their parishioners. Dr. W.A. Criswell, the famous Southern Baptist minister who preached at the historic First Baptist Church of Dallas for nearly fifty years, realized the importance of tackling the problematic passages found in the Bible. In 1971, Dr. Criswell delivered a sermon, titled "What is The Bible," that likely momentarily shook the faith of many within his congregation, most of whom had never heard a Christian, much less their conservative "Bible-believing" pastor, suggest that any part of scripture was not divinely inspired or should not be included in the Bible. Criswell said:

> When I hold in my hand this King James version of the Bible, there are some things in this text that are manifestly uninspired and

nothing but sheer unadulterated superstition. For example, in the sixteenth chapter of Mark and the eighteenth verse, Jesus is quoted as saying, "They shall take up serpents; and if they drink any deadly thing, it shall not hurt them." There is no syllable of truth in that; that is plain superstition. Alright, let us take another verse. In the fifth chapter of the Gospel of John, in explaining the miracle of the healing at the pool of Bethesda, is this fourth verse: "For an angel went down at a certain season into the pool, and troubled the water; whosoever then first after the troubling of the water stepped in was made whole of whatsoever disease he had" [John 5:4]. That is another instance of plain superstition. Nothing like that ever happened in the history of the world. Things like that, these two examples that I have read to you, are not in keeping with the Word of God: it is not the Word of God.[34]

This excerpt from Criswell's sermon is not a textual criticism argument *per se*, for his explanation for why these verses should not be included in the New Testament seemed to be based on the "superstitious" nature of the verses, not necessarily because of what the consensus of scholars have suggested based on the earliest and most reliable manuscripts. However, what is obvious by this sermon excerpt is that a staunch defender of the authority and inspiration of scripture adamantly claimed that there are a few verses in the Bible that do not belong.[35] For the vast majority of conservative evangelical Christians, many of whom revered the great Dr. W.A. Criswell as the "Baptist Pope," this suggestion could be very problematic. Criswell's sermon proves that he was not only aware of problematic passages mentioned by textual critics, but he was also willing to address the matter with his parishioners so that they could remain confident in the authority and trustworthiness of the Bible precisely because textual criticism enables

---

[34] http://www.wacriswell.org/Search/videotrans.cfm/sermon/2610.cfm

[35] It is important to note that other conservative Christian scholars believe that the longer ending of Mark does belong in the Bible because it is inspired by God.

us to know exactly what constitutes the divinely inspired words of the Bible. People can have disagreements about aspects of a particular text, but the basis on which they have those disagreements needs to be sound. Instead of rejecting any portion of the Bible because of one hang up or problematic passage, one should cautiously adopt the stance of "awaiting further light."

Unfortunately, some of today's defenders of the Bible, unlike Criswell, are not willing to entertain any of the questions posed by textual critics (that are actually footnoted in most Bibles as well), to the point that if and when other Christians engage in such conversations, suspicion or condemnation often follows. Aware of this, many conservative evangelical pastors and leaders avoid addressing issues of textual criticism, which contributes to the number of Christians who are not prepared to deal with the critics.

Unless a particular sermon passage warrants an explanation pertaining to textual criticism, it makes no sense for a preacher to bring up issues of textual criticism. However, because many churchgoers, especially high school and college students, are encountering questions and criticisms about the Bible, church leaders do need to think about ways to address the issues with their congregants. Regardless of where you might be in your study of the Bible, it would be helpful to pay attention to the notations in the scriptures, as well as consider using a study Bible and Bible commentaries to guide your learning and devotions.

Despite variants in copies of the original texts, God has perfectly conveyed what was intended through the process of textual criticism. Whenever apparent errors or problematic passages are pointed out (as with the missing fourth verse in the fifth chapter of John's Gospel), one should first establish the original context of the passage, and then analyze whether or not the story is changed as a result of the suggested omission of the text. In the case of the verse in John's Gospel, absolutely nothing of significance changes because someone suggested that the verse should be excluded. The timeless truth that God intended to convey has been preserved in the passage regardless of the exclusion of the verse. It is important to realize that a non-Christian textual critic often wants to keep the focus on the variants, whereas the Christian must strive to understand and move past them.

Looking more closely into these issues may lead to frustration or confusion, but in no way should one be concerned or lose faith because of a critic's unhealthy view of scripture or approach to textual criticism. I concur with theologian William Abraham, who wisely suggested that, "If abandoning the language of the inerrancy of scripture leads to a loss of faith, do not abandon the inerrancy of scripture."[36]

We Don't Have the Original Writings, but We Have the Original Words

No Christian should be alarmed that none of the original autographs still exist. None of the original manuscripts of other ancient writings exist either, and it is not because someone lost or misplaced them. The reason why none of the original biblical writings and non-biblical writings from the earliest centuries do not exist is because frequent usage and exposure to the elements caused the writing surfaces to erode and eventually disintegrate.

Generation after generation of Christians knew the importance of preserving God's words, and this is why so many copies of manuscripts were made and are still being discovered each year. It is of

---

[36] William J. Abraham. *The Bible:Beyond the Impasse*, 103. For a more in-depth look at inerrancy and issues related to biblical authority, see Craig L. Blomberg. *Can We Still Believe the Bible?: An Evangelical Engagement with Contemporary Questions*. Grand Rapids, MI: Brazos Press), James D.G. Dunn. *The Living Word*. Minneapolis: Fortress Press, 2009. Alvin Plantinga, *Warranted Christian Belief*. (Oxford: Oxford University Press, 2000).

utmost importance to realize that though none of the original auto-graphs exist we are now in a *better position than ever* to reconstruct with confidence the original writings of the biblical authors thanks to the discovery of thousands of ancient New Testament manuscripts that have emerged during the last century. Despite assertions that Greek manuscripts contain more than 300,000 differences, even Bart Ehrman admits that, "Scholars are convinced that we can reconstruct the original words of the New Testament."[37]

Despite only having copies of the original writings, we do have the original, divinely inspired words of the New Testament authors, thanks to the process of textual criticism.

Wasn't the Actual Content of the Bible Written Much Later?

Although modern textual criticism helps to find the original text, there are some who have a different agenda, which seeks to undermine the authority of the Bible. Critics often point out that the letters that make up the New Testament were written many years (sometimes decades) after the actual events took place.

This was not an uncommon practice during the early church era in which materials to produce writings were not readily available. There were no printing presses, copy machines, computers, note pads, external hard drives, etc. Most teaching was done by word of mouth, and in this oral culture nearly 80-90 percent of the populace could neither read nor write. Oral tradition was so prevalent, important, and reliable that many people memorized much of what they had heard. The community constantly monitored what was being read and

---

[37] Bart D. Ehrman, *The New Testament: A Historical Introduction to the Early Christian Writings*, 3rd ed. (New York: Oxford University Press, 2003), 481.

circulated to make sure that it was legitimate and accurate.

Early Christians believed the Lord's return was very near, and it is not hard to imagine why persons who saw the risen Lord Jesus did not bother writing about what was so much more easily shared by word of mouth. In the years following the resurrection, stories of Jesus's life, ministry, death and resurrection were being told and retold by those who had witnessed the most important event in history. However, as eye-witness testimonies became fewer, the need to write down and preserve what had been taught and revealed about Christ became increasingly important.

Making the Bible an Idol

Christians are often referred to as "people of the Book," which is a title that most would appreciate. However, because anything can become an idol, some Christians are guilty of Bible worship or "bibliolatry." When Christians choose to force a rigid form of interpretation (not to mention using the Bible as a manipulative tool to force people into submission), many have been led to value the text more than the actual events that took place and the God revealed in its pages. The texts bear an authoritative witness, but to make the text equal to God is to turn Christianity into a strict religion of the book that can lead to forced, incorrect readings of scripture.[38]

Scripture is divinely inspired and true in all that it teaches, but it should not be elevated above Jesus Christ, the incarnate Word to whom the scriptures bear witness. People come to know Christ through the scriptures, but it is not the Bible that forgives sinners. By clinging to ultra-rigid views of the Bible some Christians have expected too much from scripture. By placing the Bible on the same

---

[38] Robert M. Grant. *A Short History of the Interpretation of the Bible.* (New York: Fortress, 1984), 177.

59

level as its Author, Christians can run the risk of walking away from the Savior in disobedience when they run into challenges posed by critics, or even when they discover obstacles in their own reading of the Bible. This was the case for Bart Ehrman, who said, "My faith had been based completely on a certain view of the Bible as the fully inspired, inerrant word of God."[39]

It is important to realize that one can keep a very high view of scripture without utilizing the language of inerrancy in a way that is overly dogmatic or inflexible about his or her interpretation of scripture.[40] Once again, keep in mind that some Christians disagree when defining the term *inerrancy*. Even those preferring to espouse a narrow view of inerrancy have to admit that many like-minded Christians do not interpret portions of the Bible in the exact same way.

Matters become even more complex when people realize that it is impossible for every Christian to come up with the same interpretation and application of every part of the Bible. Thus, even those clinging tightly to the highest view of the scriptures have to decide how to deal with the fact that a fallible sinner will never be able to provide a perfect interpretation of the inerrant Bible. Furthermore, because the exact nuance and complexity of certain passages of the original Greek text are sometimes difficult to convey in English, learning Koine Greek could be helpful for some students. Though most choose not to learn the original languages, utilizing commentaries by respected Christian scholars can be very effective in helping one to understand the Bible.

---

[39] Ehrman. *Misquoting Jesus*, 11.

[40] Campbell. *Christian Mysteries*, 17. Howard G. Hendricks. *Living By the Book*. (Chicago: Moody Press, 1991), 25. One of the most respected and beloved Bible teachers in the past century, Howard Hendricks stated, "Inerrancy means that we have a Bible that is completely trustworthy, reliable, and without error in its original form." Biblical inerrancy has been an important and sometimes divisive topic among Christians for many years. The inception of the term occurred during the early twentieth century amid the modernist vs. fundamentalist debates that pitted science against religion and questioned the nature of the Bible.

The sixteenth-century Reformation mantra, *Sola Scriptura*, which means "scripture alone," initially appeared to be a unifying principle, yet it has created division among some Christians. This in no way means that scripture does not and should not play the ultimate authoritative role in the life of a believer and the church. It is God's Word and is absolutely essential in the daily life of a believer and the process of one becoming more like Christ (sanctification). Without divine revelation, all ground is sinking sand. Removing an authoritative role for the Bible in favor of contemporary experiences can be devastating for one's faith journey and witness, for without having the standard of scripture to keep experiences in check, chaos could ensue, which occurs when radical claims and experiences have taken place that lacked validation from scripture. The Bible is the surest way to discover the attributes of God, the purpose of creation, the sinful nature of humans, and the gospel that saves. If the Bible is not foundational for theology and praxis, then something else will be, and that can be very problematic.

Taking the Bible Literally?

Some Christians insist that everything in the Bible should be taken literally. It makes sense in most instances but simply cannot work in all circumstances. Let's take the example of Jesus making the statement, "I am the door" (John 10:9). Would not a literal interpretation of that verse mean that Jesus was a large piece of wood that was attached to a frame by hinges and moved back and forth? It may seem unrealistic to surmise that anyone would take this passage literally, but I have heard some Christians claim that every single story and passage of scripture *must* be taken literally, even though no one really interprets the Bible this way. The term *literal* comes from the Latin *litera*, meaning "letter." By paying attention to the letters and words when interpreting the Bible, the term *literally* means that a verse or passage should be interpreted according to the normal rules of grammar, speech, syntax, and context.[41] As with all forms of literature, the reader must figure out the proper genre of the biblical text.

Keep in mind that the Bible is a library of books, and therefore it is important to discover if the biblical text of the book or section being observed is a parable, poetry, history, prophecy, allegory, or something else. By first determining the genre, one can then appropriately determine what a particular book of the Bible means. One must be aware that literary devices like figures of speech, hyperbole, simile, personification, and idioms are used throughout the Bible. Failing to understand the basics of biblical interpretation (hermeneutics) can cause one's view, interpretation, and teaching of the Bible to become murky, narrow, confusing, or incorrect rather quickly.

Many scholars have suggested that when reading the Bible, one should always read and interpret scripture in light of scripture. This means that if one part of scripture appears hard to understand, there is likely another portion of the Bible that will help explain the section that was previously observed. Scripture does not contradict scripture, even if our limited understanding may assume otherwise on rare occasions. It is very important to focus on the original meaning of the text when reading the Bible. The following questions can aid in that endeavor: What was the author's intention? Who was the audience? What were the circumstances? What was conveyed? Failing to understand the genre and original context of particular parts of scripture has caused many to adopt a narrow or restrictive interpretation of the Bible.[42]

---

[41] R.C. Sproul. *Knowing Scripture.* (Downers Grove, IL: InterVarsity, 1977), 49.

[42] This is typically referred to as a grammatical-historical approach to interpreting the Bible.

It is of utmost importance to realize that there are times when orthodox Christians provide differing interpretations of the same passage of scripture. For example, a literal interpretation of the Lord creating the earth in six, twenty-four-hour periods of time makes perfect sense, even though one could suggest that the days might have been longer or *shorter* periods of time. Many Christians insist that because the Bible mentions "days" that it must be interpreted literally as twenty-four-hour periods of time, yet any Hebrew scholar will tell you that the Hebrew word used for day (*yom*) typically represented an appointed time or specific period of time, even though it may also refer to a twenty-four hour day. Because the Bible states in the creation narrative that the sun and moon were made on the fourth day, some have asked, "How should those interpreting days as literal twenty-four-hour periods of time make sense of the first three 'days' when there was no sun?" The creation narrative in Genesis is an account of a real, actual event that took place, yet the Hebrew language often describes historical events using symbolic or poetic language. Many Hebrew scholars have concluded that the days of Genesis could not refer to twenty-four-hour days based on the context and culture of the original writings.

The context determines the meaning of the word by the manner in which it is used. The debate often occurs based on how people interpret particular passages of scripture. It is important to keep in mind that God is outside of time and therefore not confined to it as humans are, for he created it and can see the present and future. No one else was present when God created the heavens and the earth. The Bible declares that, "With the Lord a day is like a thousand years, and a thousand years are like a day" (Ps. 90:4; 2 Pet. 3:8). This being the case, could not Almighty God have created everything in a matter of seconds or minutes, instead of days? Some of the most respected theologians cannot agree on the exact timeframe or way in which things were brought into existence, but clearly what matters most is that one acknowledges the Lord as the Creator.

In addition to how one views the creation narrative, other matters of interpretation can become very complicated for some Christians, and sometimes heated, when their particular view is challenged by an interpretation of scripture they do not agree with (e.g., the role of women in ministry, spiritual gifts, the end times, etc).

Eisegesis vs. Exegesis

Another problem pointed out by critics is that some Christians think the Bible was written solely for twenty-first-century readers. This presumption has caused many to interpret and apply scripture incorrectly, not to mention distorting the sacred text by reading into or projecting upon it (eisegesis), instead of interpreting only what is actually revealed in and interpreted out of the biblical text in its original context (exegesis).

Sometimes Christians try to apply a passage of scripture to modern times without first giving any reference to its original context. This often happens when preachers quote a passage and apply it to modern times without any reference to the original context of the passage. New Testament scholar Gordon Fee rightly points out, "The true meaning of the biblical text for us is what God originally intended it to mean when it was first spoken. This is the starting point."[43] Christians lose credibility when they insist on providing an answer for everything, and especially when they attempt to force the Bible to speak about matters that it does not. Referencing scripture should be based solely on what it reveals to be true, not what we want it to say.

---

[43] Gordon Fee and Douglas Stuart. *How to Read the Bible for All Its Worth.* (Grand Rapids: Zondervan, 1993), 26.

Learning to begin your interpretation with the original biblical context will only strengthen your understanding and application of the Bible. You will also notice when someone makes an incorrect reference to or commentary of the Bible (like I had done in my college literature class). It can be like hearing an opinion about a popular movie and then realizing while you were watching the movie that the secondhand information was different from what you personally observed. Let's say you are a big fan of the *Star Wars* movies and have seen every movie multiple times. If someone shared with you an incorrect recollection about a scene from a movie, you would quickly notice the error. The key is to learn how to study, interpret, and apply the scriptures, first in its original context, then to modern times.

The Self-Authenticating Nature of the Bible

Critics also point out that Christians use the Bible to validate the Bible. In order for the Bible to be the Bible it must be self-authenticating, for attempting to validate an ultimate authority by any other authority would disqualify it as an ultimate authority. We simply cannot account for God's Word as being an ultimate authority without using it to validate its authenticity. This is precisely why passages such as 2 Timothy 3:16, 2 Peter 1:21, and Revelation 22:18-19 are so important. The Bible is not self-authenticated simply because it claims to be. Rather, the Bible is authenticated as the Word of God because it bears the marks of divinity, was written by apostles and their associates, was recognized by the church in both oral and written form, and has been preserved by the Spirit that helps every generation of believers to recognize its validity and power.[44]

When we read the Bible we are reading God's words. We should

---

[44] Kruger. *Canon Revisited*, 114.

respond to it with reverence and trust. The intention of the Bible is to present the story of God's Creation and Redemption. It explains how Christians can know, love, worship, and serve God. Renowned twentieth-century minister, A.W. Tozer, put it this way:

> The Bible is not an end in itself, but a means to bring people to an intimate and satisfying knowledge of God, that they may enter into Him, delight in His Presence, and taste and know the inner sweetness of God Himself in the core and center of their hearts."[45]

In the canon of scripture we have the foundation documents of Christianity, the character of God, the formation of the church, and the title-deeds of faith. The voice of the Spirit of God continues to be heard when one reads the Bible.[46] The same Holy Spirit that enables one to embrace Jesus of Nazareth as the risen Lord and Savior also enables one to embrace the Bible as the chief means by which mankind can know Jesus and the power of his resurrection.

Approaching the Bible

The textual evidence for the reliability and trustworthiness of the Bible is unsurpassed by any other ancient manuscript. Christians can be assured that God expressed everything that was intended in the scriptures without trying to maintain that divine perfection was extended to the grammar and syntax of the written words that God inspired.[47] Even though some of the copies of the original writings contain variants, absolutely nothing to do with the message God wanted to convey is jeopardized.

Though the Bible is just as relevant today as it was when it was originally written, one should be very prayerful and careful about its

[45] A.W. Tozer. *The Pursuit of God.* (Camp Hill, PA: Christian Publications, 1993), 13.
[46] Bruce. *The Canon of Scripture*, 283.
[47] James D.G. Dunn. *The Living Word.* (Minneapolis: Fortress Press, 2009), 109.

interpretation. Though it is inerrant, not every interpretation can be. It is important to note that Christians can hold to a very high view of scripture and arrive at different conclusions when interpreting certain parts of the Bible. It is not helpful to take passages out of context to fit one's personal agenda, nor to make the Bible speak about matters on which it is silent. It really is okay for one to say, "I do not know," rather than forcing an interpretation or making the Bible address areas or things that it does not.

The questions about the Bible do have good responses that preserve the reliability and authority of the scripture. You may be asking, "What does all of this mean, and why does it matter?" It matters because at the end of the day, the Bible is completely trustworthy because it is divinely inspired by God. The evidence is overwhelmingly reliable. It has withstood the test of time. One of the most important things for Christians to remember as they delve into issues about canonization, inerrancy, textual criticism, and the nature of scripture is that there will always be some unanswered questions. There will also be times when we have to admit that we are wrong. When this is the case, keep studying, but also remember that one must walk by faith rather than by sight (2 Cor. 5:7). A person may get hung up on the number of variants, Levitical law, the book of Exodus, or someplace else, but remembering that the entire Bible is about Jesus Christ helps to regain proper focus.

Approaching the scriptures with humility is also imperative. A person can know what the Bible says, understand creeds, canonization, and the history of the church, yet still not be a Christian, or be a Christian and act very legalistic, dogmatic, judgmental, or self-righteous. This type of attitude turns off Christians, and especially people who are skeptical about the Bible and Christianity. To many non-Christians, the Bible seems weird, archaic, and irrelevant. This being the case, Christians should demonstrate humility in their approach to the scriptures and others. It is refreshing to read what the Apostle Peter once said of Paul's writings, "His letters contain some things that are hard to understand" (2 Pet. 3:16). If the scriptures somehow posed a challenge to Peter, there really shouldn't be room for the rest of us to act as if we know it all. The Bible reminds us that even Christians see through a glass dimly (1 Cor. 13:12). Imagine how much more difficult it must be for those living without divine assistance.

It is amazing to realize that a person can connect with the Creator and Sustainer of the universe each time the Bible is read. By reading the Bible, you will get to know the living God, yourself, the meaning of life, and what matters most. The Bible is not only worth reading; it will transform your thinking and living. When a person becomes a Christian and realizes that scripture is the exclusive witness to divine revelation, the invisible–Jesus Christ–becomes visible, and can be known and understood best through reading the Bible.[48] Theologian J.I. Packer sums up well how Christians should view the Bible:

> True Christians are people who acknowledge and live under the word of God. They submit without reserve to the word of God written in the Book of Truth (Daniel 10:21), believe the teaching, trusting the promises, following the commands. Their eyes are upon the God of the Bible as their Father and the Christ of the Bible as their Savior."[49]

Without the divine nourishment obtained through constant exposure to the scriptures, intellectual and spiritual malnutrition tend to follow. Warren Smith explains:

When we fail to cleave to God and open our minds to his words

---

[48] Abraham. *Crossing the Threshold of Divine Revelation*, 102.44

[49] J.I. Packer. *Knowing God*. (Downers Grove, IL: InterVarsity Press, 1975), 116.

contained in scripture, we have no roots to drink in the living water. If we do not abide in the company of the Spirit who speaks to us through the Scripture and sheds the light of divine wisdom upon our intellect, then we fail to see the world as it really is from God's perspective.[50]

True wisdom is found only in the scriptures. This is why the Apostle Paul said, in Christ "are hidden all the treasures of wisdom and knowledge" (Col. 2:3). Pursuing God is a lifelong endeavor, and there is no better aid, mentor, or road map for the journey than the Bible. Because receiving solid teaching from those who are very familiar with the scriptures should be a top priority, everyone should be part of a Bible-believing church, consider joining a small group or parachurch group, as well as gatherings that will promote serious study of the Bible. There are also a number of other helpful resources to guide one's reading and understanding of the scriptures, such as Bible commentaries, Bible dictionaries, Bible lectionaries, Bible reading plans, and sermons.[51]

The very best way to learn about God is by reading the Bible. You cannot grow in faith and spiritual maturity if you do not read the Bible. You cannot apply the truth and wisdom of the Bible to your life if you do not know what it says. If the Bible does not inform your thoughts and actions, something else will. These are but some of the reasons why you should read and study the Bible. Either the Bible is true or it is not. Either the historical events described really happened, or they did not. Either the Bible is inspired by God, and therefore trustworthy and dependable as the ultimate source for instruction, salvation, peace, and hope for this life and eternity, or it is not. The criticism and debate will never cease, but each person should reach a firm conclusion about the Bible.

---

[50] J. Warren Smith. *The Lord's Prayer: Confessing the New Covenant.* (Eugene, OR: Cascade Books), 2015.48

[51] See ligonier.org/blog/bible-reading-plans and biblegateway.com.

Questions for Discussion:

1. What is your opinion of the Bible? What, if any, role has it played in your life?

2. Why do you believe the Bible is the best-selling book in the world every year?

3. If someone asked you to explain how we got the Bible, what would you say?

4. How can we really know what the authors of scripture wrote if we only have copies of the original writings (autographs)?

5. Why do some people choose not to read the Bible?

6. What are some of the main criticisms of the Bible?

7. Why should a person read the Bible, especially since it was written so long ago?

8. If someone asked you about how to approach the Bible, what would you say?

For Further Reading

Craig L. Blomberg. *Can We Still Believe The Bible?: An Evangelical Engagement With Contemporary Questions.* Grand Rapids, MI: Brazos Press, 2014.

Gordon Fee and Douglas Stuart. *How to Read the Bible for All Its Worth.* Grand Rapids: Zondervan, 1993.

Howard G. Hendricks. *Living By the Book.* Chicago: Moody Press, 1991.

Michael J. Kruger. *Canon Revisited: Establishing The Origins and Authority of the New Testament Books.* Wheaton, IL: Crossway, 2012.

R.C. Sproul. *Knowing Scripture.* Downers Grove, IL: InterVarsity, 1977.

REJECTING GOD

What exactly is atheism? It's not just about doubting or denying God, for very few people, even the most mature believers, can avoid having doubts about God's existence at some point in life.[1] A national survey conducted in 2017 by the Barna Group revealed that two-thirds of all Christian adults had experienced doubts about their faith. One of the most important lessons learned through my college experience was that if questions remain unanswered, or are not answered sufficiently, doubt usually begins to grow. This is true for Christians, as well as those who say they don't believe in God.

I have found that most people like talking about spirituality, and that even those claiming no formal religious affiliation tend to be agnostic (uncertain but open to the possibility) about belief in God. I have also discovered that many people who deny God's existence usually have valid reasons for their disbelief. If I had to base my decision to believe in God solely on some of the personal stories told by atheists I have known, I might have a hard time believing in God as well. This being the case, it is really important to listen carefully and

[1] https://www.barna.com/research/two-thirds-christians-face-doubt/

take everyone's views about God seriously.

This chapter provides an overview of atheism, an in-depth look at a group of doubters called the "New Atheists," and ways to encourage constructive dialogue with those who do not believe in God.

The word *theism* comes from the Greek word *theos*, which means "god." A *theist* is one who believes in the existence of a god or gods, specifically a Creator or Higher Power who intervenes in the universe and other aspects of creation. You might see various prefixes used with the word *theos* to describe different kinds or versions of theists. A *mono*theist believes in one God, as seen in Judaism, Christianity, and Islam. A *poly*theist believes in many gods (e.g., the Greek or Roman gods). A *pan*theist believes that the totality of everything is or contains God—in other words, that everything is part of God. Because there are elements of pantheism in Buddhism, Hinduism, and some "New Age" or modern religious practices, followers of those religions might be polytheistic as well.

*A*theism is a system of belief that asserts categorically that there is no God, therefore the material universe, and all things it contains, was produced by chance or fate. It is sometimes referred to as "naturalism" because of its claim that all things have a natural, physical explanation. In this system of belief, the supernatural (i.e., miracles) are not possible.

Atheism is not new, and one could argue that each person is an atheist on some level. Disbelief in the existence of gods has been around for centuries. Greek philosopher Protagoras (ca. 411 BC) expressed doubt in the existence of gods, as did Greek playwright Euripides (ca. 406 BC) through many of the characters in plays.[2] In 399 BC, Socrates was convicted of being an atheist because he did

---

[2] Alex McFarland. *10 Answers for Atheists*. (Minneapolis: Bethany House, 2012), 35-51.

not believe in the Greek gods. Participants in each of the major world religions (Buddhism, Christianity, Islam, Judaism, and Hinduism) deny the gods of other religions. In the earliest days of Christianity, followers of Jesus were sometimes called atheists for rejecting the Roman emperor and other gods of society.

Given that most people deny a god or gods, and therefore could be rightly called atheists, the first question to consider when one claims to be an atheist is, "Which gods does the atheist not believe in?" The next question for consideration is, "Why has he or she not come to believe in God?"

There are many reasons why people do not believe in God. The most common reason results from growing up in an environment where others did not believe in God. During my first day on the job at an Episcopal school, a student approached me and asked, "Are you the new chaplain?" I replied, "Yes," and he said, "Cool, because I'm an atheist." I then responded by saying, "Great, I'll look forward to getting to know you and discovering how you arrived at your belief system." It was refreshing to serve in an environment where students felt comfortable enough to ask questions and express beliefs that ran counter to the majority.

Through our subsequent conversations, the student came to realize that his atheism had more to do with his upbringing (both parents were atheists) than what he actually knew and believed about Christianity. Two years after our first conversation, and just one week prior to his high school graduation, I asked the student if he was still an atheist. I'll always cherish his response. He said:

> I'm actually agnostic now, and I'm looking forward to continuing the search for truth. I'm grateful to have been in an environment that encouraged me to ask questions, share my doubts, and figure out my own beliefs. It was easy to deny God when my Christian

friends seemed to be saying one thing, and then living in a way that contradicted their beliefs, but watching my teachers live out what they claimed to be true about God has made me more open to the possibility of believing in God.

Each of us is on a journey, and there are few things more important than encouraging people to figure out what they believe and why they believe it.

Many people do not believe in God because of negative encounters with people who do. I have friends who grew up in the church but no longer want anything to do with organized religion. Some claim to be spiritual, but not religious, like famous bass player, Flea, of the alternative rock band the Red Hot Chili Peppers, who said: "I love God, but I don't trust religion."[3] For people who have only experienced an unbiblical version of God (portrayed as a cosmic Cop or angry Judge who is impossible to appease), abandoning their negative perceptions makes perfect sense. For those who have been manipulated or abused by a person claiming to be religious, their rejection of religion is also understandable.

Some other reasons why people do not believe in God include: the undeniable existence of evil and suffering in the world (which is dealt with in the next chapter), to remove guilt associated with religion, to eliminate fears of a judgment or hell, and to avoid the moral challenges of the Christian tradition.

Though disbelief in a god or gods has been around for centuries, the remainder of this chapter will focus on atheists who believe there is no god at all. This brand of atheism has existed for several centuries, during what has been called the modern era.

---

[3] https://hollowverse.com/flea/

Modern Era Atheism

Much of modern era atheism is the continuation of what started during the Enlightenment period more than 200 years ago, when proponents of "deism" came on the scene. Deists believed that God created the world but left his creatures to fend for themselves and make the most of the situation, sort of like a divine clock-maker who creates a clock, sets things in motion, and goes away for good. Belief in rationalism and common sense became the real religion among some who claimed to be Christians. Many were skeptical about the supernatural, which explains why Thomas Jefferson chose to omit accounts of miracles in his revised personal New Testament known as the "Jefferson Bible."[4]

Leaving aside the differences within the Enlightenment period that spanned the seventeenth and eighteenth centuries, one of the primary goals was to implement rationalism (human reason) and empiricism (experiences) to replace traditional religious beliefs as the best way to acquire knowledge. In other words, people were to be reasonable and base everything on science (oftentimes what could be perceived through the senses) and common sense rather than divine revelation.[5] The hope was for war and strife to decrease and peace to prevail.

Precisely the opposite has taken place since the late eighteenth century, as God went from being viewed by Enlightenment thinkers as a distant deity to completely ignored in some circles. Over time, many people realized that science may teach us how to create or understand

---

[4] The Jefferson Bible is on display at the Smithsonian National Museum of American History.

[5] Rene Descartes (ca. 1650), the first modern philosopher, and author of *Meditations*, along with Baruch Spinoza, (ca. 1677), author of *Ethics*, were the two leading rationalists of the seventeenth century. Skeptic Philosophers David Hume (1711-1776) and Immanuel Kant (1724-1804) are considered by many to be the pioneers of modern atheism for proposing that all knowledge is derived from sense-experience.

things but not how to use them properly. Those skeptical about God were still left with the challenge of making sense of a world that has no explanation for what's wrong or how to fix it. Consequently, many who had embraced deistic or atheistic leanings during the Age of the Enlightenment still respected those who believed in God and still acknowledged Christianity's contribution to the world.

During the early to mid-twentieth century, atheists Jean-Paul Sartre and Albert Camus attempted to articulate the tension between humanity's desire for God to exist while living in a meaningless and hopeless world. Without God, the "absurdity of life" was conveyed through novels like Camus's *The Fall* and *The Plague*, or plays like Sartre's *No Exit* and Samuel Beckett's *Waiting for Godot*. These existentialist philosophers appeared to have a basic understanding of Christianity and the claims of the Bible. Though they disagreed with theists, civil discourse was usually possible.

Not all of the modern era atheists have chosen to curb their criticism of Christianity. At times the cultural cynicism and mistrust toward religious institutions and adherents were justified, and some atheists rightly exposed much of the corruption. Eighteenth-century French philosopher Voltaire was very critical of Christianity and often claimed that the attractiveness of atheism was directly dependent upon the corruption of Christian institutions.[6] During the late nineteenth century, philosopher Friedrich Nietzsche declared, "God is dead." He elaborated on his pronouncement in a writing called *The Antichrist:*

> I condemn Christianity; I bring against the Christian Church the
> most terrible of all the accusations that an accuser has ever had in
> his mouth. It is, to me, the greatest of all imaginable corruptions; it

---

[6] Alister E. McGrath. *The Twilight of Atheism: The Rise and Fall of Disbelief in the Modern World.* (New York: Doubleday, 2004), 27

seeks to work the ultimate corruption, the worst possible corruption. The Christian Church has left nothing untouched by its depravity; it has turned every value into worthlessness, and every truth into a lie, and every integrity into a baseness of soul.[7]

Clearly, Voltaire and Nietzsche felt compelled to blast Christianity based on negative personal experiences, particularly corruption within the church. Perhaps the resentment was justified, but one can't help but wonder what version of Christianity would drive someone like Nietzsche to write books condemning the faith of his father and grandfathers, all of whom were Lutheran ministers. For many atheists who have spoken out against God or Christianity, the explanation or justification for their actions often resulted from negative experiences with religious people. In order to grasp the depth of such resentment, it might be helpful to explore what some have labeled "the Atheist Syndrome."

The Atheist Syndrome

Some have asked, "What could cause so much intolerance and hatred for religion?" The answer may lie deep within some of the most passionate proponents of atheism. It has been noted that many of the most influential modern era atheists experienced childhood interpersonal trauma accompanied by attachment insecurity that typically resulted from abusive or negligent parents, especially fathers.[8] John Koster has labeled this unfortunate trend "the atheist syndrome" and builds a compelling argument by describing the childhoods of Charles Darwin, Thomas Huxley, Friedrich Nietzsche, and Sigmund Freud.[9]

[7] Quoted by John C. Lennox. *Gunning for God: Why the New Atheists Are Missing the Target.* (Oxford: Lion Hudson, 2011), 64.

[8] Paul Vitz. *Faith of the Fatherless: The Psychology of Atheism.* (San Francisco: Ignatius), 2013. John P. Koster. *The Atheist Syndrome.* (Brentwood, TN: Wolgemuth & Hyatt), 1988.

[9] Koster, 16.

Similarly, Paul Vitz shows in *The Faith of the Fatherless* that a significant part of the atheist position has been an aggressive interpretation of religious belief arising from psychological factors, not the nature of reality.[10] Vitz charts the lives of some of the most influential atheists to support his thesis: Joseph Stalin was severely beaten by his alcoholic father who also beat his mother, and Adolf Hitler had been the victim of severe beatings by his father as well.

Paul Johnson's book, *The Intellectuals*, also sheds light on how abusive and overly religious parents often pushed their children and grandchildren into the direction of atheism.[11] Johnson explains how Karl Marx and his Jewish parents became Protestants because Prussian law banned Jews from law practice, and that Karl had been so abused by his father that he did not bother to attend his funeral. Johnson also describes how abusive parents pushed Jean-Paul Sartre and Bertrand Russell toward atheism.[12]

There are, of course, exceptions to the trend, but Koster, Vitz, and Johnson make a compelling case for the link between the resentment, mistreatment, or the absence of fathers with those who have become the most outspoken and influential atheists during the past two centuries. The evidence helps one to understand how easy it might be for a child who experienced abuse from an earthly, religious parent to end up despising or not believing in a heavenly Father. Christians need to realize that many people who do not believe in God have understandable motives for their disbelief.

---

[10] Vitz, 4.

[11] Paul Johnson. *The Intellectuals: From Marx and Tolstoy to Sartre and Chomsky.* (New York: Harper, 2007), 201, 226.

[12] Ibid, 74. It is worth noting that Sartre denounced atheism and embraced God while on his deathbed.

The New Atheism

In recent decades, a "new atheism" has emerged that differs from the unbelief espoused by previous generations of atheists in a variety of ways. Unlike most of their modern era atheist predecessors, some contemporary atheists are angry, aggressively outspoken, and typically ill-informed about the Bible and Christianity. They are often dismissive and intolerant of most religious people and determined to convince everyone of the need to eradicate the world of religion altogether.

In 2002, an estimated 20,000 atheists and skeptics gathered on the US Capitol lawn in Washington D.C. for the Rally for Reason conference. Keynote speaker Richard Dawkins, a former professor of science at Oxford University, personally helped finance the gathering, as well as subsequent events promoting atheism in recent years. Dawkins, along with Daniel Dennett, a philosophy professor at Tufts University, the late Christopher Hitchens, and neuroscientist Sam Harris make up a group of aggressive, sometimes militant, atheists who are often referred to as the "New Atheists." These dogmatic defenders of secular orthodoxy are occasionally referred to as the "four horsemen of the apocalypse" because of their campaign to rid the world of religion. They are opposed to religion in general and Christianity in particular, and they have worked tirelessly through lectures, debates, and books, hoping to create an atheist revival by spreading the gospel of unbelief. Each of the four horsemen has sold thousands of books, often landing on the *New York Times* best-seller list, expanding the message of evangelical atheism, not to mention their bank accounts.

Atheists view humans as merely products of evolutionary means, without any divine Creator. Because they process and analyze the world and human behavior through evolutionary lenses, religions are viewed like harmful biological traits that can mutate and spread.[13] This is one reason why the New Atheists view religion as a type of virus or disease that has affected the weak-minded masses. Both atheists and theists realize that human nature is flawed or broken, but the approaches to remedy the problems are radically different. Aggressive atheists believe that removing God and religion (the viruses) will improve the situation, whereas Christians believe that only God can eliminate the real problem (sin) that plagues everyone (2 Cor. 5:21).

From the start, the New Atheists' agenda has been to replace a religious worldview (way of looking at the world) with a secular, naturalist one. Sam Harris states, "My goal is to get Americans to value the principles of reasoning and educated discourse that now make a belief in evolution obligatory."[14] The late Christopher Hitchens desired nothing more than for Americans to join the ranks of the unbelievers, or "nones," which some studies have shown to be the fastest-growing minority group in the United States.[15] With similar intentions, Richard Dawkins stated in the *The God Delusion* that he hopes all religious readers who open his book "will be atheists when they put it down."[16]

Because the New Atheists believe that religion has done more harm than good, society has no place for God. Sam Harris in *Letter to a Christian Nation* stated, "The primary purpose of this book is to arm secularists in our society, who believe that religion should be kept out of public policy."[17] It is not about equality or neutrality, but replacing

---

[13] Jonathan Haidt. *The Righteous Mind: Why Good People Are Divided by Politics and Religion.* (New York: Vintage Books, 2012), 295-96.

[14] Sam Harris, *Letter to a Christian Nation.* (New York: Vintage Books, 2008), 175.

[15] Hitchens, *God is Not Great: How Religion Poisons Everything.* (New York: McClelland & Stewart, 2008), 286. In 2005 the Pew Center for Research concluded that 23 percent of the US population claimed no formal religious affiliation. This group has been referred to as the "nones." See pewresearch.org

[16] Dawkins, *The God Delusion.* (Boston: Houghton Mifflin, 2006), 5.

[17] Harris, *Letter to a Christian Nation*, viii.

one agenda with another. Prominent social critic Os Guinness explains that by denying God, each alternative worldview becomes "a shrine to the self that raises a shelter from the truth of God that atheists would avoid. In short, moral, social and philosophical fictions are raised to replace what would have otherwise been the undeniability of God's truth."[18] By denying or suppressing God's standard, substitute standards usually fill the gap in the form of a "new religion." This explains why the elimination of religion has been the primary goal of the New Atheists.

The freedom to believe or not believe in God is a privilege that should be extended to all people. As a general rule, all beliefs should be respected. In their defense, it is an unfortunate fact that atheists have experienced discrimination over the centuries, especially when running for political office or other positions of influence. Sadly, rather than fighting for equality, the New Atheists have labored to eliminate freedom of religion. Trading one form of discrimination for another is not the answer, yet Sam Harris admits wanting "to destroy the intellectual and moral pretensions of Christianity in its most committed forms."[19] One should not be misled into thinking that eliminating "religion" will somehow create universal tolerance, acceptance, peace, and freedom for everyone to enjoy. It will not work, for when truth is suppressed and exchanged for lies, freedom eventually vanishes (Rom. 1).

Douglas Murray, himself an atheist, explains in his best-selling book *The Madness of Crowds* how the dismantling and destruction of traditional religious and political ideologies has enabled the adoption of radical agendas to prevail, most of which are more complex, restrictive, and unstable than many are willing to admit. Murray warns

---

[18] Os Guinness. *Fools Talk: Recovering the Art of Christian Persuasion.* (Downers Grove, IL: InterVarsity, 2015), 152-153.
[19] Ibid, ix.

that "there is something demeaning and eventually soul-destroying about being expected to go along with claims you do not believe to be true and cannot hold to be true."[20] Forcing people to believe in a god, atheism, or anything else for that matter, should not be tolerated.

The Atheist Belief System

Like Christianity, atheism is a belief system that requires faith. Ironically, many atheists beg to differ. Christopher Hitchens once stated of the New Atheists, "Our belief is not a belief, and our principles are not a faith."[21]

Oxford professor John Lennox pointed out the error in such reasoning: "The New Atheists do not seem to realize that everyone has a worldview, for there is no neutral position."[22] Every person makes and lives by exclusive truth claims. An atheist can say, "I don't believe in God, and Christians are making exclusive truth claims." This is true, but that simple statement of disbelief pronounced by the atheist is also an exclusive truth claim. Because every worldview begins with faith in something, the question is not if New Atheists believe, but in whom or in what they believe. Lennox goes on to explain:

> It is impossible to live either intellectually or emotionally in a completely god-less world. Deliberately or subconsciously, even atheists fill the vacuum left by their dismissal of the one true God with all kinds of substitutes. Centuries of experience have shown that the question is not whether you will believe in God or not, but whether you will believe in the one true God who claims to have made you,

[20] Douglass Murray. *The Madness of Crowds: Gender, Race and Identity.* (London: Bloomsbury Continuum, 2019), 9.

[21] Sam Harris. *The Moral Landscape: How Science Can Determine Human Values.* (New York: Free Press, 2010), 5.

[22] John Lennox. *Gunning for God: Why the New Atheists Are Missing the Target.* (Oxford: Lion Hudson, 2011), 63.

or in one or many of the other things which you have made your substitute gods.[23]

Many New Atheists have chosen science as their substitute god. Dawkins clearly demonstrates faith in science and is adamant about judging those who don't share his belief. Dawkins stated, "It is absolutely safe to say that if you meet somebody who claims not to believe in evolution, that person is ignorant, stupid or insane."[24] Similarly, Sam Harris demonstrates his faith in naturalistic evolution:

> All complex life on earth has developed from simpler life-forms over billions of years. This is a fact that no longer admits intelligent dispute. If you doubt that human beings evolved from prior species, you may as well doubt that the sun is a star.[25]

It is important to understand the difference between naturalistic evolution and theistic evolution. Atheists believe in naturalistic evolution—that humans are the product of an undirected, accidental process because God does not exist. Further, naturalistic evolution proposes that humans evolved from other species (macroscopic evolution). Though many Christians believe in microscopic evolution (like bacteria becoming resistant to antibiotics), the vast majority reject macroscopic evolution, as well as the idea of theistic evolution (that God used evolution to create humans). Naturalistic evolution contradicts the Bible, for the scriptures make clear that God is intimately involved in the creation and development of humans (Jer. 1:5; Ps. 139:13-16). Theists point to both the Bible and nature as evidence for an intelligent, divine Creator, whereas atheists believe that creation can be explained apart from God.[26]

[23] David Gooding & John Lennox. *Key Bible Concepts.* (Coleraine, Ireland: Myrtlefield House, 2013), 3-4.

[24] Quoted in Alex McFarland. *10 Answers for Atheists: How to Have an Intelligent Discussion About the Existence of God.* (Minneapolis: Baker House, 2012), 69.

[25] Harris, *Letter to a Christian Nation,* 68.

[26] Michael G. Strauss. *The Creator Revealed: A Physicist Examines the Big Bang and the Bible.* (Bloomington, IN: WestBow Press, 2018), 134-140.

What atheists like Harris and Dawkins claim as facts are actually proposals requiring faith, and the explanations given for their scientific beliefs have often been lackluster and unconvincing. For example, the atheists' worldview still tends to require a belief in eternal things (e.g. matter, energy and/or the laws of physics) but views all gods as figments of theists' imaginations. Christians believe that God is uncreated and has existed eternally as the creator of all things. So ultimately atheists would rather point to everything having a natural and undirected cause despite the abundance of evidence that points to an intelligent Designer.

When pressed for an explanation, the vast majority of atheists offer theories for creation that appear less credible than what many religions have claimed. Richard Dawkins, when asked for his theory about the inception of the universe, pointed to "the origin of the first self-replicating molecule." Regarding the origin of human life on earth, Dawkins said:

> It could be that some earlier time, somewhere in the universe, a civilization evolved by probably some kind of Darwinian means to a very, very high level of technology and designed a form of life that they seeded onto this planet. That is an intriguing possibility. I suppose it is possible that you might find evidence for that if you look at the B cells of molecular biology."[27]

When listening to Dawkins explain the origin of the universe and humanity, one can argue that it takes more faith to be an atheist than to believe in a Creator.

---

[27] Richard Dawkins interviewed by Ben Stein. https://www.youtube.com/watch?v=12rgtN0pCMQ

Atheist Fundamentalists and Critiques of Christianity

Some have labeled the New Atheism a zealous form of fundamentalism.[28] These critics point to the New Atheists' intolerance, hasty generalizations, usage of scare tactics, failure to understand their opponents, and conviction that they are intellectually superior and in sole possession of the truth (scientific or otherwise).[29] Ironically, fundamentalist versions of religion, with which the New Atheists have so much in common, are the very targets of their attacks. The worst actions committed by people of faith (e.g., extremist suicide bombings or abuses by clergy) are often mentioned as if representative of all people serious about belief in God. Seldom are traditional, orthodox structures of religion acknowledged or intellectual Christian apologists referenced. Instead, the New Atheists typically mention fringe, radical groups to caricature all religious people. Despite most people realizing that peripheral extremist groups do not represent the religions of the masses, the New Atheists' strategy has been to keep the focus solely on religious crimes and misrepresentations, casting all religious people in a negative light.

Another unfortunate and dishonest strategy of the New Atheists has been the deployment of scare tactics to convince people that there is imminent danger looming because of religion. Following the terrorist attacks in 2001, the New Atheists rightly pointed out the dangers of radical religion. However, they have often erred by assuming that all

---

[28] The term *fundamentalist* was originally given to evangelical Christians who adhered to the fundamentals of the faith during the early twentieth century. Today the term often refers to conservative evangelical Christians who are viewed as being overly zealous, dogmatic, and sometimes anti-intellectual. The term has also been applied to any religious person holding extremist views. See David Bentley Hart. *The Atheist Delusions: The Christian Revolution and Its Fashionable Enemies.* (New Haven: Yale University Press, 2009).

[29] See Amarnath Amarasingam. *Religion and the New Atheism.* (Chicago: Haymarket, 2011).

religious people are dangerous extremists. Daniel Dennett in *Breaking the Spell* opines that, "The current situation is scary—one religious fanaticism or another could produce a global catastrophe."[30] Sam Harris claims that, "Some propositions are so dangerous that it may even be ethical to kill people for believing them."[31] Christopher Hitchens states, "Religion poisons everything. As well as a menace to civilization, it has become a threat to human survival." He concludes his warning by claiming, "As I write these words, and as you read them, people of faith are in their different ways planning for your and my destruction."[32]

Some religious radicals do have the intention of causing harm to others who do not share their beliefs. But the exact same logic can be applied to atheists who seek to harm others, not to mention the millions of murders that occurred in the twentieth century that resulted from atheist regimes (Stalin, Mao, Pol Pot, etc.). For the New Atheists to suggest that all religious people belong in a category with religious zealots, and that all religion is poisonous, is misleading and wrong, just as it would be for a theist to label all atheists as uncivil, uncaring, radical, or dangerous. These flagrant misrepresentations reveal both a lack of reasoning and a lack of basic religious awareness.[33]

Rather than being a menace to society, it could be argued that the vast majority of religious people strive to make the world a better place. Though Christianity is not a western invention, western civilization with its justice system, civil rights, and basic human values all have their origin from Christianity, yet atheists oddly ignore these facts as well. While there are legitimate and understandable reasons why some have shunned religion, most people, regardless of their

---

[30] Daniel Dennett. *Breaking the Spell: Religion As A Natural Phenomenon.* (New York: Penguin, 2007), 310-311.

[31] Sam Harris. *The End of Faith: Religion, Terror, and the Future of Reason.* (New York: Norton, 2006), 52.

[32] Hitchens, *God is Not Great*, 13, 25.

[33] Ravi Zacharias. *Beyond Belief: Living the Truth We Defend.* (Nashville: Thomas Nelson, 2007), 30.

religious affiliation, are in fact better neighbors and citizens because of their faith. Failing to mention the many good things in society that religiously motivated people produce is clearly one of the blind spots of the New Atheists, akin to Christians failing to acknowledge that some atheists have made remarkable contributions for the betterment of mankind.

Sometimes it seems easier to criticize others, especially when one has been hurt or wronged, than to acknowledge our own shortcomings. Everyone has blind spots. Atheist Bertrand Russell once said, "The Christian religion, as organized in its churches, has been and still is the principal enemy of moral progress in the world."[34] There is no doubt that people of various faith backgrounds have done foolish, selfish, and evil things in the name of their religion, but let us not forget the countless positive contributions that have resulted because of religion, particularly Christianity, such as the establishment of universities, hospitals, orphanages, the Red Cross, Salvation Army, and many other humanitarian organizations. We should not easily ignore the undeniable positive contributions done in the name of Christ.

Another common tactic of the New Atheists' campaign has been to label theists as intellectually inferior or insane. Daniel Dennett boasts of being a "bright" person who strictly adheres to a naturalistic worldview, as opposed to credulous, religious simpletons who believe in the supernatural. Dennett asserts, "We brights don't believe in ghosts or elves or the Easter Bunny—or God."[35] Similarly, Sam Harris writes, "The boundary between mental illness and respectable religious belief can be difficult to discern."[36] Richard Dawkins labels theists as "delusional" and their forms of indoctrination as "child abuse."

---

[34] Betrand Russell. *Why I Am Not a Christian*. (New York: Touchstone, 1957), 21.

[35] https://www.nytimes.com/2003/07/12/opinion/the-bright-stuff.html

[36] Harris, *The End of Faith*, 184.

Dawkins also states that anyone refusing to believe in evolution is "ignorant, stupid, or insane."[37]

Labeling all theists as intellectually inferior or mentally ill should cause one to question the seriousness and sincerity of the accusers. Outspoken critic of religion, NYU professor Thomas Nagel, offers a more candid analysis: "I want atheism to be true, and am made uneasy by the fact that some of the most intelligent and well-informed people I know are religious believers."[38] If and when believers on college campuses or in workplace settings are made to feel like someone cannot be an intelligent Christian, keep in mind that some of the most brilliant and influential people in the world believe in God.

The number of towering Christian intellectuals is mind boggling.[39] Studies have shown that 40 percent of scientists believe in God, yet the New Atheists want people to believe that one cannot be both a good scientist and a theist.[40] Christian physicist John Polkinghorne of Cambridge and philosopher Richard Swinburne of Oxford are two of the most influential intellectuals of the past half century. Oxford mathematics professor John Lennox and widely respected historians George Marsden, Mark Noll, Grant Wacker, and Dana Robert have made indelible contributions through their respective academic positions. Intellectuals Vishal Mangalwadi, Alvin Plantinga, and Ravi Zacharias have gone toe to toe with foremost philosophers across the globe. Francis Collins leads the National Science Foundation Gene Institute. Fred Brooks at the University of North Carolina is a world- class computer

---

[37] Richard Dawkins. "Put Your Money on Evolution," *The New York Times*, April 9, 1989.

[38] Quoted by Peter Hitchens. *The Rage Against God: How Atheism Led Me to Faith.* (Grand Rapids: Zondervan, 2010), 150.

[39] In the area of literature alone, one would be hard pressed to deny the intellect and contribution of writers such as George McDonald, G.K. Chesterton, J.R.R. Tolkien, C.S. Lewis, and Dorothy Sayers.

[40] https://www.nytimes.com/2005/08/23/us/scientists-speak-up-on-mix-of-god-and-science.html
https://journals.sagepub.com/doi/full/10.1177/2378023116664353

scientist and Nobel Laureate. Newspaper magnate Walter Hussman has epitomized ethical journalism for decades. David Brooks and Ross Douthat are leading columnists for *The New York Times*. Peter Hitchens (brother of the late New Atheist, Christopher Hitchens) is a brilliant author and journalist. John Grisham, Dave Ramsey, and J.K. Rowling are but a few of the world's best-selling authors year after year. The list of influential Christians goes on and on.

It does not take long for one to realize that many of the New Atheists either have, or choose to use, a selective or superficial understanding of Christianity and history. At the same time, Christians must realize that one of the main reasons why their contributions go unnoticed is because too few are impacting the world beyond their concentric circles of like-minded Christians. If Christians want to dispel the perception of being intellectually inferior and culturally irrelevant, they must produce excellent work that is deemed worthy of the highest standards.

Atheist Theologians

Though atheists claim not to believe in God, most are happy to provide an opinion of him. Dennett, Dawkins, and Harris spend much time elaborating on their understanding of the Bible and Christianity, yet seldom provide an accurate account of what the Bible states or what Christians actually believe. For example, Dawkins attributes the letter of Hebrews to the Apostle Paul, which has not been the consensus for centuries.[41] Not only are numerous interpretive errors of scripture presented by Dawkins throughout *The God Delusion*, but he often cites people like fictional writer Dan Brown and other skeptics instead of credible biblical scholars to support his arguments. By far

---

[41] Dawkins, *The God Delusion*, 287.

the most ill-informed claim posited by Dawkins, Hitchens, and their atheist predecessor Bertrand Russell is that Jesus of Nazareth likely never existed.[42] Very few credible historians of antiquity deny that Jesus lived, and even agnostic New Testament scholar Bart Ehrman has presented overwhelming proof that the historical Jesus lived during the first century.[43]

It is difficult to take seriously the criticism of a scientist like Dawkins posing as a biblical expert who describes the Bible as a "plain weird, chaotically cobbled-together anthology of distorted documents, composed, revised, translated, distorted and improved by hundreds of anonymous authors, editors and copyists, unknown to us and mostly unknown to each other, spanning nine centuries."[44] David Bentley Hart explains how Sam Harris, in a similar fashion, "displays an abysmal ignorance of almost every biblical topic he addresses—Christianity's view of the soul, its moral doctrines, its mystical traditions, its understanding of scripture, and so on."[45] In *The Moral Landscape* Harris states, "It makes no sense at all to have the most important features of our lives anchored to divisive claims about the unique sanctity of ancient books or rumors of ancient miracles."[46] One does not have to view the Bible and Christianity as being true, but any credible Bible scholar or historian of antiquity can easily see through the one-sided, naïve, and often perverted view of the Bible and Christianity that is often being promoted by the New Atheists.

---

[42] Ibid,122. Hitchens, *God is Not Great*, 114. Russell, *Why I'm Not a Christian*, 16.

[43] Bart Ehrman. *Did Jesus Exist?: The Historical Argument for Jesus of Nazareth*. (New York: HarperOne), 2013.

[44] Dawkins, *The God Delusion*, 268.

[45] David Bentley Hart. *The Atheist Delusions: The Christian Revolution and Its Fashionable Enemies*. (New Haven: Yale University Press, 2009), 8.

[46] Harris. *The Moral Landscape*, 25.

Misunderstanding Faith and Science

The myth that science and religion are incompatible has existed for centuries, and both atheists and Christians have sometimes failed to realize there can be more than one level of explanation for things pertaining to the material universe. Sixteenth-century scientist Galileo Galilei, who eventually came to be regarded as the "father of modern science," espoused theories contrary to those of the church (though the church's ideas were not based on a proper understanding of what the Bible actually says about these scientific ideas). His rejection of the popular Aristotelian view (that the Earth was at the center of the universe) and promotion of Copernicus's heliocentrism (that the earth and planets revolved around the sun) went against the grain of the established norms at the time, yet he was willing to risk rejection to follow the evidence wherever it led him.

Once Galileo's discovery became widely accepted, some questioned not only the church, but the God of the church as well. Questions were raised about what other mistakes Christians might be making. In this case, Christians were mistaken as to the order of the solar system because of the misunderstanding of what the Bible claims, and atheists erred in assuming that Galileo's discovery disproved the existence of God.

The problem with the recent criticism brought by the New Atheists regarding the church's ignorance and dogmatic stance on issues related to science in the past is that they ignore the fact that the church's historical stance at the time was valid based on the knowledge then available. Generations of atheists have failed to emphasize Galileo's commitment to orthodox Christianity and that his discovery, rather than disproving the existence of God, served only to strengthen his faith in the Creator.

Two lessons can be learned by this illustration. First, science can change. Second, Christians need to be careful about their interpretation of scripture, especially when trying to use the Bible to speak about matters that it does not specifically address. Recall the discussion in the previous chapter about always reading the Bible in its original context first. In this case, previous generations of Christians had made the mistake of trying to use the Bible as a science textbook. The sixteenth-century reformer John Calvin was well aware of this danger when he stated, "If you want to learn about astronomy, you should ask the astronomers, not Moses."[47]

Since the opposition of the New Atheists in the name of science has become one of the main attacks on Christianity, believers should be aware of their basic criticisms and assumptions. Modern scientists like Richard Dawkins and the late Stephen Hawking have often been chief among those claiming a breach between scientific explanations about how the universe operates and belief in a god who designed and sustains it. Like their atheist predecessors, Hawking and Dawkins have claimed that one must choose between God and science, and that when trying to understand something like Isaac Newton's law of gravitation, God should no longer be acknowledged. Both Hawking and Dawkins have acknowledged Newton's explanation of gravity as valid, but neither believe that God created or sustains gravity.

While atheists choose to believe that everything came from nothing, and that elements of nature function perfectly without cause or explanation, theists realize that the natural sciences often provide direct evidence for the existence of God (Ps. 19:1; Rom. 1:20). Renowned particle physicist Mike Strauss, in his book *The Creator Revealed,* does an excellent job explaining the coherence of science and religion:

---

[47] John Calvin. *Commentary on Genesis.* (Grand Rapids: Baker, 1981), 1:86.

No matter where we find truth, we will discover something about the God of all truth. Christians, more than any other people, should be searching for truth wherever it may be, whether it is found in the Bible, in astronomy, in psychology, in geophysics, or in any other area. We should never be afraid that accurate knowledge or understanding of something might lead to a newly discovered truth that will destroy our faith. Since we serve the God of all truth, we can be sure that any truths we find will support the foundational knowledge that God has revealed himself, rather than destroy what we believe.[48]

It all comes down to acknowledging that all truth is God's truth and being willing to follow the evidence wherever it leads. Strauss sees no conflict between science and religion because God is the Creator of both.

Religious Secularism

Secularization can be defined as the process by which religious ideas and institutions lose their social significance. Not all secularists are atheists, but they do operate as if God should play no significant role within society. Most atheists believe that humans, instead of God, are to shape and control the ethos of society, communities, institutions, etc. As secularists, the New Atheists have a clear, unified agenda—the push for secularization and the marginalization of people of faith.

This agenda has been most noticeable at colleges and universities, even those institutions founded on Christian beliefs. One does not have to look very hard to see how secularization has sidelined Christianity. Countless private schools (elite high schools and universities alike) have chosen to abandon their original religious commitments for the sake of "academic credibility" or the pressure to balance budgets

---

[48] Strauss. *The Creator Revealed*, 113-14.

and adopt progressive cultural norms, and, sadly, most have done so at the expense of losing, or distancing themselves from, their religious heritage. Historian George Marsden's book, *The Soul of the American University,* explains how the majority of Ivy League schools, such as Harvard, Princeton, Yale, and Brown were founded specifically to train ministers but gradually abandoned their Christian mission.[49]

Today, the situation in some parts of academia is such that when people refer to God in any serious way, the legitimacy of their scholarship can be called into question. People should not have to apologize for their differences, especially when their religious beliefs in no way alter or compromise the integrity of education. Universities, of all places, should encourage discussions regarding differences of opinion. Why deprive students of the opportunity to hear different voices and find common ground that can serve as a platform for more in-depth dialogue in the pursuit of truth?

The *Merriam-Webster* dictionary defines *tolerance* as, "Sympathy or indulgence for beliefs or practices differing from or conflicting with one's own."[50] Discrimination against religious people has often been couched within new policies designed to promote tolerance. Ironically, some of the greatest advocates of "tolerance" have shown the least amount of tolerance for people who do not share their ideology. Numerous religious groups throughout the nation have been marginalized or completely ousted for not adhering to new rules stemming from secularization.[51] Places where the free exchange of

---

[49] George Marsden. *The Soul of the American University: From Protestant Establishment to Established Nonbelief.* (Oxford: Oxford University Press, 1996). Essentially all of the Ivy League schools have drifted from their explicit Christian heritage.

[50] www.merriam-webster.com

[51] A simple Google search leads to dozens of examples of Christian groups that have been ousted at colleges like the University of Michigan, University of Iowa, Duke University, and Vanderbilt University. There are usually two sides to every story, but it will be interesting to see what happens when schools start trying to ban groups affiliated with other religions.

ideas used to be the norm are becoming increasingly harder to find. Identity politics has restricted freedom of speech at some colleges to the point that even a number of famous comedians have refused to perform at campuses anymore.[52] Some students have been led to believe that anyone who disagrees with their ideologies, preferences, view of history, or religion might be hateful or racist. Some people have been reprimanded, silenced, and in some cases forced into conforming with things they fundamentally cannot believe.[53]

It's one thing to disagree, and another to force people (through intimidation, bullying, or false accusations) to believe and practice things that contradict their convictions. Everyone needs safe spaces so that constructive dialogue and the ability to learn from others sharing differing opinions can occur. Without such spaces, it can become difficult for people to learn how to disagree without demonizing others. When people of faith, regardless of their religious affiliation, are not allowed the freedom to experience spiritual integration within their jobs, schools, and other public spaces, everyone loses (including atheists).

Ask people in other parts of the world whether or not they would appreciate the ability to voice and live out personal convictions that run contrary to others, and you will be reminded about the liberty that generations of Americans have experienced because of religious freedom. Despite this reality, some secularists remain steadfast in their determination to diminish religious liberty. Attempting to eliminate religion from the public sphere does not help civil discourse, for freedom of religion, regardless of one's worldview, is a privilege that should be cherished and championed by all people. In recent years, even Richard

---

[52] Jerry Seinfeld, Chris Rock, Dave Chappelle, and Pete Davidson have all chosen to limit appearances because of increasing hypersensitive politically correct (PC) cultural restrictions. https://www.hollywoodreporter.com/news/jerry-seinfeld-political-correctness-will-800912

[53] The movie *No Safe Spaces* highlights the danger of eliminating free speech.

Dawkins has admitted that eliminating Christianity might actually lead to something even less appealing filling the void.[54] Only by promoting true religious freedom will genuine tolerance take place.

Responding to the New Atheism

Since we've summarized much of their approach, how should well-meaning believers respond to the New Atheists, especially since theists and atheists see themselves as possessing an ultimate truth? Atheist Sam Harris seems eager to find out: "So let us be honest with ourselves: in the fullness of time, one side is really going to win this argument, and the other side is really going to lose."[55] Obviously, both cannot be right, but they can learn from one another. Despite the counterproductive combativeness of both the New Atheists and some Christians, both groups should stop caricaturing and polarizing one another.

Both groups are setting up false dichotomies that can only damage the cause of biblical and scientific literacy; undermining honest, constructive dialogue; and ultimately perpetuating the seemingly endless culture war. In fact, some of the ways in which Christians approach non-Christians in their "witnessing" can result in more harm than good, especially when people come across as being condescending, arrogant, impatient, or super spiritual. I've known too many Christians who go on and on about God's grace but demonstrate so little of it. I've also known atheists and agnostics who do not know how much they are loved because they have only been made to feel judged or inferior by Christians.

Additionally, creating and knocking down straw men does not help

---

[54] See October 5, 2019 "Ending Religion Is A Bad Idea." www.thetimes.co.uk
[55] Harris, *Letter to a Christian Nation*, 2.

either side. I have seen too many second-rate "Christian" movies and books that caricature atheists in unfair ways, while atheists return the favor and portray Christians inaccurately. Both groups need a dose of humility and education regarding what each group actually believes. Many people need to learn how to disagree without vilifying others. Don't ever forget that all are equal and created in the image of God, and that understanding and embracing the gospel should matter more than anyone's view of creation, eschatology, or any other secondary matter.

The real frustration for many atheists has more to do with religious people than the gods they represent. In this regard, the criticism of Christians by atheists should not be ignored. The late Christopher Hitchens provided some good advice that Christians should take to heart. Reflecting on his numerous debates promoting atheism around the world, Hitchens made two keen observations: "Christians are un-used to debate, and are surprised by how many people are impatient with them, or even scornful."[56] At another point in his *New York Times* best-selling book, Hitchens, frustrated by his opponent's ignorance of Christian doctrine, opines, "I run into this all the time. What else do people imagine they are believing? Hasn't it come to something when I have to tell Catholics what their church teaches?"[57]

In the final paragraph of his book, Hitchens sheds more light on the anemic state of cultural Christianity prevalent throughout much of America—"Everywhere I speak, I find that the faithful go to church for a mixture of reasons, from social to charitable to ethnic, and take their beliefs a la carte or cafeteria-style, choosing bits they like and discarding the rest."[58]

Hitchens is correct. If Christians are to be taken seriously, then

---

[56] Hitchens. *God is Not Great: How Religion Poisons Everything,* 290.

[57] Ibid.

[58] Ibid, 293.

they need to seriously study the Bible, church history, and views of their critics, for only then will they be able to understand and relate to the culture in which they seek to transmit the Good News of Jesus Christ.

Before Christians can properly respond to the questions posed about the faith, they need to answer them for themselves.[59] This means that having a basic understanding of the Bible, creeds, doctrine, and church history is essential. History is full of examples for people to emulate. Austin Farrer, one of the most respected Anglican priests of the twentieth century, understood the importance of knowing scripture and learning from previous generations of saints: "We can often learn more about God from St. Paul and St. Augustine than we can from our own lives."[60] A half century ago, Bertrand Russell called out Christians for their shallow understanding of Christianity:

> The word Christian does not have quite such a full-blooded meaning now as it had in the times of St. Augustine and St. Thomas Aquinas. In those days, if a man said that he was a Christian it was known what he meant. You accepted a whole collection of creeds which were set out with great precision, and every single syllable of those creeds you believed with the whole strength of your convictions.[61]

Unless Christians take the time to understand scripture and the fundamentals of orthodox Christianity, as well as the basic criticisms being leveled by the defenders of secularism and unbelief, they will not be able to identify and expose the flaws that are leading people away from faith, nor give people a compelling reason to consider Christianity.

---

[59] Alister E. McGrath. *Mere Apologetics: How to Help Seekers and Skeptics Find Faith.* (Baker Books: Grand Rapids, MI, 2012), 18.

[60] Austin Farrer. *God is Not Dead.* (New York: Morehouse-Barlow, 1966), 116-117.

[61] Russell. *Why I Am Not a Christian,* 4.

A Way Forward

God has been using atheists to challenge and grow the faith of Christians for centuries. Instead of shying away from difficult topics and questions, we should be embracing them. If one's faith is so fragile as not to entertain questions and criticism, then he or she probably needs to rethink their beliefs. It is time for all of us to take our faith, and the views of those with whom we differ, much more seriously. By familiarizing ourselves with the most popular atheists' writings, (both old and new), Christians can develop a better understanding of the main arguments being posed, as well as how to respond most accurately.

The most effective response can only occur when Christians have carefully examined what the skeptics actually believe, not just what has been assumed or said about them. The story of the Apostle Paul speaking in Athens is an example to emulate. Paul was familiar with the many gods and objects of worship that dominated the culture in which he ministered. Because Paul understood and respected the beliefs of people with whom he fundamentally disagreed, he was eventually given an opportunity to share his beliefs. Scripture reveals that some became followers of Christ and that others requested another opportunity to hear Paul's teaching (Acts 17:16-34).

The Apostle Peter was clear about the expectations Christians should have in terms of their witness: "Always be prepared to give an answer to everyone who asks you to give the reason for the hope that you have. But do this with gentleness and respect (1 Peter 3:15)." "Being prepared" shouldn't mean being ready to belittle or argue someone into belief in God. That approach seldom leads to constructive conversations, much less convincing someone of their need for Christ. If you are a Christian, how many times has someone asked you for the reason for the hope you have? How often have you responded with gentleness and respect? The relationship should always be about respect and healthy dialogue, not winning an argument.

As you spend quality time with people and ask great questions, you might be surprised by how inaccurate your preconceived ideas of others might actually be. Through genuine relationships, Christians will be able to understand why certain people have chosen not to believe in God, and also may be given opportunities to dispel the inaccurate assumptions that others have about Christianity.

I am amazed by how many college students are eager to challenge my faith and engage in transparent conversations. I have also been amazed by how many people in the public square share their disdain for Christianity. This should not anger, discourage, or intimidate Christians in any way. In fact, the New Atheism should awaken believers to the great opportunity and responsibility they have been given to see, love, and treat people the way that Christ does.

Because asking good questions can raise other questions, one should consider a list of questions to facilitate constructive dialogue with the hope of leading others to the logical consequences of their beliefs. Some helpful questions are:

How do you think the universe and humans came into existence?

What is your view of sin, death, and life beyond the grave?

Do you believe in some form of god, higher power, or intelligent designer?

Do you consider yourself a spiritual person?

Have you ever had a spiritual or supernatural experience?

Also, be sure to ask about the evidence backing truth claims and how one arrived at a particular conclusion. Even atheism requires faith and is itself a type of belief system. Like some Christians who cannot explain why they believe in God, there are atheists who cannot explain why they don't. Rather than accepting the "faith" of your childhood, investigate the claims of both atheism and Christianity, and be willing to go wherever the evidence leads.

It would be wise to heed the advice given by my college professor: "If you are going to be a Christian, then be a good one, or if you choose to be an atheist, then be a good one." Either choice requires faith, and genuine faith lived out consistently is difficult to dismiss. When one notices a Christian's life aligning with the scriptures being proclaimed, Christianity becomes more attractive.

Being an effective witness for Christ can only occur through intentional relationships. The sad reality is that most Christians have very few non-Christian friends, and part of the reason is because they do not know how to relate to people who are not Christians. This unfortunate trend can change if Christians will be more open and intentional about getting to know non-Christians. If Christians remain in their "holy huddles," it will be much easier for those who do not understand the gospel to remain in their ignorance and sins.

It is important to meet people where they are, really listen, and get to know them. At some point you will discover how they arrived at their belief system, and eventually they will inquire about yours. What people really need to know is that someone sincerely cares, and most importantly, that God cares for them. What people really need to see is genuine faith lived out on a consistent basis.

Along with developing friendships and transparent dialogue, Christians should realize that debate, disagreement, and occasional arguing may take place in their daily journey as ambassadors for Christ. The Lord's brother, Jude, urged Christians to "contend for the faith that was once for all entrusted to God's holy people" (Jude 1:3). The Apostle Paul once said, "Be prepared in season and out of season; correct, rebuke and encourage—with great patience and careful instruction" (2 Tim. 4:2). Remember Peter's charge to respond with "with gentleness and respect" (1 Pet. 3:15). Seldom are people argued into belief, but there is a way to approach the topic. The word *argue* generally invokes fear and negativity, yet God's grace can enable Christians to face challenges to their faith, even hostility toward their beliefs, in a way that is reasonable and informed, rather than taking the objections personally and responding in a defensive, ignorant fashion.

Gregory Koukl, in his engaging book, *Tactics,* points out that "those who refuse to dispute have a poor chance of growing in their understanding and defense of the truth. The ability to argue well (with gentleness and respect) is vital for clear thinking. It is also a virtue because it helps us determine what is true and discard what is false."[62] Providing a safe environment in which disagreements and debate can occur should enable true maturation and unity to develop and serve to strengthen each person's beliefs and ability to articulate them well.

Oftentimes misconceptions, prejudices, and negative feelings toward Christianity result from ignorance—ignorance of God, the Bible, ourselves, and the beliefs of others. If you create opportunities for differences to be voiced and truly heard, you might be surprised to discover how often God tends to show up in those moments. By carefully listening, genuinely caring, and conveying beliefs in a respectful way, people learn how to agree to disagree, while becoming better classmates, co-workers, friends, or neighbors in the process. It also affords the opportunity for the truth to be heard.

Theists and atheists will continue to disagree about whether or not God exists. They can argue all day long about how creation occurred, where humans came from, who determines morality, and what is the

[62] Gregory Koukl. *Tactics: A Game Plan for Discussing Your Christian Convictions.* Grand Rapids: Zondervan, 2009, 33

meaning of life, but everyone should be concerned with whether or not there is life beyond the grave, for death is certain and no one can escape it. If atheists are right, and this life is all there is or ever will be, then everyone should just enjoy their time on earth and not give eternity another thought. However, if Christianity is true, and death is the entrance to eternity, can one afford to be wrong about it? Why take the chance?

Everyone bases their life on something. Science is a valuable tool that helps us know how many things work, yet science cannot answer the most important questions, such as, "Why are we here and what is the meaning of life?" Each person should decide what to believe about whether or not God exists, what should matter most in life, and what may exist beyond the grave. According to the Bible, without God's grace we're all doomed to an eternity without hope (Eph.2:1-10). Christians have been given the opportunity and mandate to share the reason for the hope that is within them. Christ's command to make disciples, known as the Great Commission, isn't supposed to be something Christians participate in only when it's convenient (Matt. 28:18-20). In Romans 10:14-15, the Apostle Paul's challenge to believers:

> Everyone who calls on the name of the Lord will be saved. How,
> then, can they call on the one they have not believed in? And
> how can they believe in the one of whom they have not heard?
> How beautiful are the feet of those who bring the good news!

Sometimes Christians share the gospel, but people don't actually hear it, and therefore cannot believe it, because of the way in which it was conveyed. If Christians come across as being arrogant or holier-than-thou, why should those outside of Christ want to have anything to do with them or the Christ they represent? Pointing a finger or barking a scripture verse at non-believers doesn't work either. Rather, Christians must first convince them of God's love, power, grace, and holy will, for God alone can forgive sins and provide ultimate peace.[64] One of the most important questions for a Christian to consider each day is, "How am I loving people who do not know Christ?"

The Christian response to atheism, secularism, or anything else that seems to contradict the truth of Christianity should not be defensive or reactionary, but eager to engage with gentleness, respect, and truth. Remember that one who is put off with religion may very well have valid reasons for rejecting it. Atheism often results from bad experiences with Christ's followers more than what the Bible and tradition actually teach. Hopefully, Christians will take atheism and other worldviews seriously, listen carefully to criticism, respond in humility, and rely on the Spirit, so that the gospel will be communicated with intelligence, meekness, clarity, and power. Rather than being worried or frustrated by criticism and attacks leveled by skeptics, Christians should embrace it as an opportunity to help people realize how much the God they don't believe in really does love and care for them, and longs for them to seek forgiveness and acknowledge him as the Lord of their lives.

---

[64] Austin Farrer. *Saving Belief.* (New York: Continuum, 1994), 79.

Questions for Discussion:

1. What are some of the main reasons why people do not believe in God?

2. Why do you believe, or not believe, in God?

3. What makes the "New Atheists" different from previous generations of atheists?

4. What can Christians learn from atheists?

5. What can atheists learn from Christians?

6. What did Peter mean by giving a defense for faith, but doing so with gentleness and respect?

7. How might you be more intentional about relationships with people who hold different religious views or do not believe in God?

For Further Reading:

John Lennox. *Gunning for God: Why the New Atheists Are Missing the Target*. Oxford: Lion Hudson, 2011.

Alex McFarland. *10 Answers for Atheists: How to Have an Intelligent Discussion About the Existence of God*. Minneapolis: Bethany House, 2012.

Alister E. McGrath. *The Twilight of Atheism: The Rise and Fall of Disbelief in the Modern World*. New York: Doubleday, 2004.

Randy Newman. *Questioning Evangelism: Engaging People's Hearts the Way Jesus Did*. Grand Rapids: Kregel, 2017.

SPEAK OF THE DEVIL

When you think about the devil, what comes to mind? Perhaps a cartoon character, a historical event like the Salem Witch Trials or a movie such as *The Conjuring* or *The Blair Witch Project* or *The Exorcism of Emily Rose*?

For nearly two millennia, the world has been saturated with references to the devil and the demonic, and many Christians have taken the reality of Satan very seriously. Historically, Christians have typically been the ones to affix the term *devil* both to people and ideologies they deemed evil—from Martin Luther labeling the Pope as the devil's spokesman, to governments and politicians describing their opponents as being "of the devil." Differing world powers have sometimes referred to one another as "the Great Satan." Paintings, sculptures, movies, songs, poems, novels, plays, and even sports mascots have depicted the devil in a variety of ways. Some references have been subtle, while others quite obvious. Did you realize that simply adding the letter *d* to the word *evil* forms the word *devil*? Now you do.[1]

Sometimes the devil has been mocked and at other times feared

---

[1] Thanks to Catholic theologian and friend Peter Kreeft for pointing this out to me.

or ignored. During the Middle Ages, many Christians believed that poking fun at the devil and evil spirits would repel their presence, which is why gargoyles were placed within the beautiful architectural structures of many churches, especially those designed in the Gothic fashion. Scary carved jack-o-lanterns originally stood guard during Halloween for similar purposes.

The devil has long been a central figure in the thoughts and writings of Christian theologians.[2] St. Augustine's *City of God* portrays the battle between the heavenly city ruled by God and the earthly city where the devil reigns. John Bunyan's classic allegories, *The Pilgrim's Progress* and *The Holy War*, assume the reality of the devil and his enmity for humankind. For eighteenth-century pastor Jonathan Edwards, the greatest philosopher of Puritanism, Satan was just as necessary for explaining evil and human history as the Prince of Darkness in John Milton's *Paradise Lost*.[3] Generations of ordinary Christians have believed that daily life consists of humans caught in the middle of the cosmic battle between God and Satan, and that except for God's restraining grace, everyone would be swayed and eventually destroyed by the devil.

In more recent years, however, disbelief in Satan has spread faster than disbelief in God, and the number of people who actually believe in a literal devil has decreased with each passing generation.[4] Written at the end of the twentieth century, Andrew Delbanco's seminal book *The Death of Satan* described the devil's diminishing influence on American culture and the void left behind:

---

[2] Key figures in the history of Christianity have devoted portions of their writings to the demonic, including Justin Martyr, Origen, Athanasius, Augustine, Aquinas, Luther, Calvin, Karl Barth, and C.S. Lewis.

[3] George Marsden. *Jonathan Edwards: A Life.* (New Haven, CT: Yale University, 2004), 167.

[4] Andrew Delbanco. *The Death of Satan: How Americans Have Lost the Sense of Evil.* (New York: Farrar, Straus, and Giroux, 1995). See also William J. Abraham. *Shaking Hands With the Devil: The Intersection of Terrorism and Theology.* (Dallas: Highland Loch Press, 2013).

The work of the devil is everywhere, but no one knows where to find him. We live in the most brutal century in human history, but instead of stepping forward to take the credit, he has rendered himself invisible. Although the names by which he was once designated (in the Christian lexicon he was assigned the name Satan) have been discredited to one degree or another, nothing has come to take their place. Yet, something that feels like this force still invades our experience, and we still discover in ourselves the capacity to inflict it on others. Since this is true, we have an inescapable problem: we feel something that our culture no longer gives us the vocabulary to express.[5]

According to Delbanco, though the devil is all around us, most fail to notice, much less take seriously, the possibility that a real devil exists.

Modern references to the devil have often been a far cry from the depictions of the past. What previous generations tried to avoid, modern culture has embraced as entertainment. One popular philosopher of modern culture, Mick Jagger of the Rolling Stones, wrote the smash hit "Sympathy for the Devil" in 1968. In 1976, the song "Ave Santani," from the movie *The Omen*, won the Academy Award for best original score. The rock band Motley Crue's best-selling album *Shout at the Devil* gained the attention of adoring fans in the 1980s, not to mention many parents who hoped the band members were not actual devil worshippers. In hindsight, it may seem easy to dismiss a rock band as having merely staged a controversial persona in order to boost record sales, but what are we to make of some of the current influences that celebrate or idolize occult practices, suicide, drug abuse, promiscuous, and detrimental behaviors?[6]

During the past few decades, many of the top-grossing movies and

---

[5] Ibid, 9.

[6] Two television series in particular, *Evil* and *13 Reasons*, have been both popular and controversial.

best-selling books have focused on the topic of angels and demons.[7] Examples seem endless, and as long as society continues to crave and consume this type of "entertainment," the production of similar works will continue. Some seem harmless enough, while much has led to disturbing thoughts and behavior. Beyond the desire to increase ratings or make more money, what encourages the production of dark and morbid entertainment coming out of Hollywood at an increasing rate? Perhaps there is more going on than we realize.[8]

More Than Meets the Eye

The fact that devils are predominantly comic figures in the modern imag-ination will help you. If any faint suspicion of your existence begins to arise in his mind, suggest to him a picture of something in red tights, and persuade him that since he cannot believe in that, he cannot believe in you. – from C.S. Lewis's *The Screwtape Letters*

Conversations about the devil, angels, and demons can get com-plicated and weird rather quickly, but they are usually interesting. Sometimes it is easier to make fun of things we don't understand or want to be true. I remember Dana Carvey's popular character "Church Lady" on *Saturday Night Live* who was often interviewed about cur-rent events and always found a way to blame the devil for just about everything. Whether it was bad weather, a bad hair day, politics, or

---

[7] At the box office, *The Exorcist* made $232 million, *The Conjuring* made $137 million, and *The Nun* grossed $117 million.

[8] It can be easy for modern readers to dismiss references to a spiritual world, especially anything de-monic, if they are aware of reports that turned out to be bogus. The "Satanic Panic" movement of the 1970s and 80s is a prime example. Anton LaVey's *Satanic Bible*, the popular *Exorcist* movie based on William Blatty's best-selling novel, and former Satanist-turned-preacher Mike Warnke's book, *The Satan Seller*, caused many credulous people to believe fabricated stories that eventually were proven false. Because some Christians believed, spread, or manipulated the hype, some people have chosen to ignore the possibility of the supernatural, and especially a devil.

a favorite team losing a game, audiences roared with laughter each time the Church Lady said, "Could it beeeeee SATAN?"

Sadly, I've come across some real "church ladies" along the way. I'm talking about those self-righteous, culturally detached Christians who tend to act paranoid, superstitious, and downright wacky as they try to categorize everything as directly related to the devil with themselves as his constant target. I have no doubt there are spiritual battles going on, but sometimes one's circumstances are not demonically derived. I've heard Christians blame the devil for their frustration and misfortune instead of realizing that their circumstances may have resulted from bad decisions, sin, or the practical consequences of living in a fallen world.

But on the other end of the spectrum are people who will not believe anything unless it can be explained or proven by natural causes, even though some things occur that simply have no natural explanation (we will look at some examples in a moment). Ignoring, denying, or rationalizing the spiritual realm does not make it cease to exist. Everyone is influenced by the spiritual world whether they realize it or not, and some believe that the demonic can be most powerful when people are least aware of its presence. That includes Delbanco, who writes, "If and when the reality of evil and the demonic escape our imagination, it will have established dominion over us."[9]

The modern author who stirred my own interest in the demonic was the British academic and apologist C.S. Lewis. As it turns out, God also used Lewis's writings to help my oldest son consider the immaterial world—and to help me realize the need for Christian parents to take these discussions seriously. I'll never forget the day that he came home having just participated in a discussion of C.S.

---

[9] Delbanco, 234.

Lewis's classic book *The Screwtape Letters*. This perennial best-seller describes the fictional correspondence between a senior demon, Uncle Screwtape, and his nephew, Wormwood, just as the young demon begins his role as a tempter. The teacher asked the students—all attendees at a Christian school in a very religious part of the country—if they believed in a literal devil. My son reported that no one raised a hand, and that some of the students laughed about the question, while others began referencing Hollywood portrayals from movies like *The Exorcist* and *Hellboy* and the television series *Lucifer*.

As he provided other examples mentioned by his classmates, it dawned on me that Hollywood addresses things that many churches do not, and if preachers, parents, and teachers are not willing to educate people about this subject, someone else will. As we continued the conversation, I could tell that my son, who has attended Bible-believing churches and great Christian schools his entire life, seemed uncertain about the existence of a literal devil, so I asked him what he thought about *The Screwtape Letters* in general, and if he could relate to a particular part of it. I had assumed that given how often we had prayed as a family, discussed scripture, attended church, referenced sermons, and talked about spiritual things, that my son would have no question about whether or not his greatest Enemy actually exists. I was caught off guard by his very next question: "Dad, is there really an invisible battle going on, with real demons and a real devil trying to tempt and distract me and others from knowing and serving God?" This chapter is the answer to his question.

The reality is that we are living at the intersection of visible and invisible worlds, and even people with no formal religious affiliation recognize that supernatural forces exist. It is the reason why billions

---

[10] This line has been mentioned by many over the years, perhaps most recently in the movie, *The Usual Suspects*.

of people claim to be spiritual, religious, or interested in paranormal activity. Americans are fascinated by the spiritual world, whether they believe that it actually exists or not. Ask some of your friends, colleagues, coworkers, or neighbors if they are superstitious, consider themselves to be a spiritual person, believe in a spiritual realm or practice any form of spirituality, and you'll receive all sorts of interesting answers. It seems that most people believe in the supernatural, and many want to talk about it, even if they remain agnostic about the Bible or Christianity. James Hetfield, the iconic frontman of the famous heavy metal band, Metallica, when asked if he believed in God, responded, "I believe in a higher power. Yes. I don't know, he, she, it, whatever, I see it everywhere. It is everything to me. If I choose to see it, it makes me feel better."[11] Hetfield is not alone, for most people embrace some form of religion because it makes them feel better.

Suffice it to say that most people have an opinion of the spiritual realm, and that their view of it plays an important role in their life. Various forms of the "New Age" movement, many of which essentially deny a transcendent God in favor of each person becoming a god (or one with "God"), have become commonplace in many major cities, especially among people under forty. There is also a growing interest in witchcraft, "the wellness revolution," various forms of magic, uses of crystals, channeling, mediums, and the like.[12] I remember a couple of my acquaintances during college participating in Wicca and other forms of "spirituality," but it seems that what used to be isolated to a small minority has become increasingly popular among young adults in recent years. Did you know that there are more than a million

[11] https://metalheadzone.com/does-james-hetfield-believe-in-god-or-higher-power/

[12] *Los Angeles Times,* "How Millennials Replaced Religion with Astrology and Crystals," July 10, 2019. *The Washington Post,* "The Wellness Revolution Has Reached Its Shamans-For-Hire Stage," October 3, 2018. *The Austin Chronicle.* "Austin Witches Circle: It's Not a Coven, It's a Community," September 29, 2017.

self-professed witches living in America today?[13] Theologian N.T. Wright believes that, "The main reason why witchcraft has been allowed to spread in the Western world is because some people choose to believe that it does not exist, while others regard all religious experience, however bizarre, as a private matter which is of no concern to anyone save the practitioner."[14] It shouldn't be too surprising, for witchcraft, sorcery, and various kinds of magic are mentioned in the Bible and have existed for thousands of years (Lev. 19:31; Deut. 18:11; 2 Chron. 33:6; 1 Sam. 15:23, 28:5-10; Gal. 5:18-21).

Countless people have had supernatural experiences (both good and evil) that cannot be explained in any other way, and many have no problem devoting their faith and attention to such things.[15] Some people are fascinated by evil because they have been drawn by its power or what appeared to be beautiful. Others view all of it as mere entertainment. Horror movies in particular have become year-round offerings. Despite the popularity, some people believe movies and books of this nature should never venture beyond the world of make-believe. When "real life" experiences are reported, skeptics dismiss the claims as having resulted from primitive superstition, attention seeking ploys, mental disorders, hallucinations, or drug abuse. This may be the case in some situations, but can every one of the thousands of stories be dismissed or explained by natural causes? Popular national op-ed columnist Ross Douthat explains the mentality of those who believe in the supernatural:

---

[13] *Newsweek,* "Number of Witches Rises Dramatically Across the U.S. as Millennials Reject Christianity," November 18, 2018. See also Steven D. Smith. *Pagans and Christians in the City: Culture Wars from the Tiber to the Potomac.* (Grand Rapids: Eerdmans, 2018).

[14] Tom Wright. *Spiritual and Religious: The Gospel in An Age of Paganism.* (London: Hodder & Stoughton, 1992), 52.

[15] https://www.nytimes.com/2018/12/12/opinion/christianity-paganism-america.html

If you want to understand what, if anything, a person *means* when he says he believes in demons or angels or ghosts, the simplest baseline answer is this: He means that if confronted with an encounter or an experience that seems demonic or ghostly or angelic and asked to rationalize it, he will be inclined to give credence to the possibility that the encounter is, in fact, what it appears to be.[16]

People certainly don't have to understand or agree with the assertions or explanations provided by "spiritual" or religious people, and many will not, but for those who have had an undeniable encounter with the supernatural, particularly angels or demons, there is simply no better explanation.[17]

Encountering Angels

Until a few years ago, I thought of the spiritual world much as I did the good and bright side of the Force. The good vs. evil portrayed in the *Star Wars* movies had informed my thoughts and understanding of the actual spiritual realm. I had no trouble believing in angels, and even thinking that I may have encountered them on several occasions, but rarely had I considered the existence of demons, which are actually rebellious or "fallen" angels. The word *angel* means "messenger," and the Bible provides many examples of their existence.

It seems that angels are always near, whether we realize it or not, for the Bible declares that angels are sent forth as God's messengers to minister to believers (Gen. 28:12; Heb. 1:14). They are spiritual beings that can occasionally reveal themselves in bodily form (Matt. 28:5; Heb.13:2). The Apostle Peter stated that angels "are stronger

[16] https://www.theatlantic.com/personal/archive/2008/12/gods-and-monsters.html Accessed April 8, 2019
[17] See Malachi Martin. *Hostage to the Devil: The Possession and Exorcism of Five Contemporary Americans.* (New York: Harper One, 1999).

and more powerful" than humans (2 Pet. 2:11). We don't know how many angels exist, but the Bible mentions that there are "thousands of thousands" of angels (Ps. 68:17; Heb. 12:22). The examples provided throughout the scriptures are plentiful and fascinating. An angel shut the mouths of lions to protect the prophet Daniel in the lions' den (Dan. 6:22). Angels freed the apostles from prison (Acts 12:15). Angels announced the birth of Jesus, and they were present throughout his life, including when he was tempted by Satan in the desert, prayed in the Garden of Gethsemane, and at his resurrection (Matt. 4:11, Luke 2:9-14, 22:43, John 20:10-17). Angels will also be present at Christ's second coming (Matt. 25:31).

There has been some debate about whether or not people should talk or pray to angels, even though this practice has been part of the Catholic, Greek Orthodox, and other Christian traditions for centuries. Many of my Catholic friends claim that each person has been assigned a guardian angel and have pointed to Matthew 18:10 as the basis for their belief.[18] Some of these friends have admitted to talking and praying to angels. This may seem odd to non-Catholic Christians (Protestants), but one could argue that it isn't much different than sharing a prayer request with a trusted friend. Peter Kreeft, one of the most insightful and respected philosophers of the past half century, makes some interesting claims about both angels and demons:

> Angels are present, right here, right now, right next to you, reading these words with you.…You really do have your very own "guardian angel." Everybody does.… Angels are bodiless spirits, with intelligence, and will, live in God's presence in heaven, obey his will, carry his messages, assume bodies as we assume costumes, and move material things supernaturally.… There are also evil angels, fallen angels, demons or

---

[18] Matthew 18:10 states, "See that you do not despise one of these little ones. For I tell you that their angels in heaven always see the face of my father in heaven."

devils. These too are not myths.... They can pervert God's revelations or deceive us with false revelations. They can tempt us through our imagination and feeling, and occasionally can even move matter supernaturally.... All orthodox Christians believe the teachings of the Bible, and angels are clearly taught throughout the Bible.[19]

Believing that each person has a personal guardian angel, that we should talk or pray to angels, or that angels and demons supernaturally move physical objects on occasion, are topics that various Christians may have to agree to disagree on. One thing on which all Christians should agree is that the Bible commands us not to worship angels (Col. 2:18). Though angels may be superior and more intelligent than humans, they are also created beings who are subordinate to their Creator and are therefore not to be worshipped.

Because angels exist and are aware of us, it would make sense for people to assume their presence and believe they can interact with humans, just as they ministered to and encouraged Jesus at times throughout his earthly ministry (1 Cor. 4:9, 1 Tim. 5:21). I have no doubt that these invisible agents of God can interact with the physical world and sometimes appear in bodily form. I have taken comfort in hearing stories of angelic intervention told by people I respect. My good friend Lynn once described how an angel helped her escape great danger when walking home from church on a Sunday evening while living in New York City. Lynn was alone and had noticed that a pretty rough-looking guy with some type of cane started following her just as she passed him. As she sped up, the loud tapping of his cane on the sidewalk made her aware of his fast encroachment. Lynn turned around just in time to notice her attacker had raised his cane to strike her in the head. From out of nowhere, in what seemed to

---

[19] Peter Kreeft. *Angels and Demons: What Do We Really Know About Them?* (San Francisco: Ignatius, 1995), 17.

be happening in slow-motion, a stunningly beautiful woman with slick white hair, dressed entirely in white, ran between her and the assailant to stop the blow of his cane. The attacker fell down, got up and ran away. The heroic figure never paused. Lynn hurried home, fully convinced that an angel had protected her.

I also remember a fascinating story told by Dale Earnhardt Jr., NASCAR'S most popular driver for many years, which aired on *60 Minutes* in 2008. You might want to watch the interview using the link provided in the footnote section on the next page. While racing a Corvette on a practice course in Sonoma, California, cameras captured Earnhardt's Corvette crash and burst into flames. The interior camera angle of the car revealed that Earnhardt was dazed and unable to move as the flames flashed around him. An exterior camera angle showed Earnhardt moving backwards out of the car and then being attended by crewmen as he lay dazed on the ground before being airlifted to a nearby hospital. He suffered multiple burns and bruises and recalled just being thankful to be alive. What Earnhardt shared next during the interview left the reporter, and likely many others, trying to make sense of what really happened. Earnhardt recalled crashing, passing out momentarily, and that he was eager to thank the man who saved his life by pulling him out of the car.

The exterior camera angles did not show anyone assisting him out of the car. The interior camera revealed that he remained motionless as flames engulfed his car. Earnhardt recalled how someone grabbed him under the arms and lifted him out of the car, and he adamantly wanted to thank the person who saved his life. He also remembered becoming quite upset when told repeatedly that no one had helped him escape. When asked by the reporter to explain what happened, Earnhardt implied that an angel, or his deceased father, somehow helped him to safety.

There is no reason for me to doubt that an angel appeared to my friend Lynn in private, or in the situation involving Dale Earnhardt Jr. that aired on national television.[20] It has always been easier for me to believe in stories of this nature than the ones related to the dark side of the spiritual realm. Each time I heard stories regarding demons and spiritual warfare over the years, I was usually a little skeptical about most examples, as well as the people sharing them, until my own personal encounter.

Facing the Demonic

Several years ago, I planned a speaker series event that featured Irish Methodist theologian, William "Billy" Abraham, discussing how experiences with supernatural evil led him to belief in God. Knowing there would be some skeptics and agnostics in attendance the next evening, I began praying for the event—especially for the people who had expressed doubts about Christianity and were planning to attend. For some reason, I remember feeling distracted as I was praying before going to bed. After the "amen" and having slept peacefully for several hours, I was awakened by what sounded like someone opening our bedroom door. A glimpse of light coming from the hallway enabled me to see the shadow of the extremely large figure that was standing at the foot of our bed. All I knew to do was throw the covers off the bed and lunge at the intruder. As I jumped over the footboard, my startled wife shouted, "What are you doing?" I yelled out, "Turn on the light, there is someone in the room!" When the light came on, what I had seen was no longer visible.

While searching the bathroom and closet, we heard a noise coming from our oldest son's bedroom. I rushed to the doorway and realized

---

[20] https://www.youtube.com/watch?v=PRWgXLPfsr8

that he was having a bad dream. As he tossed and groaned, I sat on the edge of the bed and whispered the assurance that everything was ok. When I prayed over my son, a calmness filled the room as he returned to a peaceful sleep. As my wife and I began to process what in the world had just happened, we heard our youngest son coming down the hallway. With his teddy bear under one arm and tears coming down his cheeks, he said, "I had a bad dream. A really big snake was chasing me." We assured him that everything was alright and then prayed him back to sleep. I would love a reasonable, natural explanation for what happened that night. It was more annoying and frustrating than scary, and I doubt we will ever know what really took place.

The speaker series event the following evening attracted a larger crowd than expected, and what was scheduled for an hour and fifteen minutes lasted more than two hours. No one left. Professor Abraham's testimony and follow-up answers were extraordinary. Most in the room would attest to the undeniable presence of the Lord that evening. As Billy and I took in a late dinner following the event, I shared with him the details of our family's bizarre experience the night before.

I'll never forget his response, nor the tone in which he said it: "I hope you are always aware of the presence of evil, for spiritual warfare is real. If you are not aware of it and the tension it can create, you might need to think about how you are living and what you are pursuing. This is serious, and I will certainly pray for you and your family. I'm so glad that you seem convinced of the Enemy's presence, because now you will be better prepared for the on-going battle."

Bad vs. Evil People

Perhaps you've heard similar stories or experienced situations when beings from the invisible world seemed to manifest themselves within the visible world. If so, you are certainly not alone, for there have been thousands of credible stories shared about encounters with both angels and demons. It can be easy to dismiss faked stories and Hollywood portrayals, but what are we to make of the real-life stories that we hear about from time to time, especially the ones told by people we respect? As real and convincing as many of the stories may seem to be, some people still refuse to believe in the supernatural, especially the demonic.[21] This being the case, let's approach the topic from another angle.

I think most would agree that there is a difference between bad and evil people. Everyone faces the daily issues and challenges of living in a broken world. Everyone is prone to think, say, and do the wrong things at any given moment. We are born with faulty wiring. The Bible declares sin to be part of our inherited human nature, and because we are sinful people, we need God's grace to guide our daily lives (Rom. 3:10-12, 23). Even if you don't believe in the Bible, I have no doubt that you believe in evil people.

Let's face it—you and I are flawed people who have both demonstrated and experienced bad behavior at times, but what constitutes "evil" behavior belongs in another category. It has been said that evil people possess the same sinful nature as the rest of us, but they are actually being influenced by supernatural forces that most observers cannot fathom or detect. They have a morbid view of humanity and are often driven by sinister motivations that you and I cannot comprehend (e.g., Hitler, Stalin, Charles Manson, Ted Bundy, etc.). They are not only capable of evil, but they actually long for the demise of innocent people. Things that sane people would deem as horrific and unimaginable, evil people have been known to enjoy. Some have claimed

---

[21] Famous atheist psychiatrist Sigmund Freud denied the supernatural, and therefore labeled "demon possession" as a mental disorder. Freud's student, Carl Jung, however, was open to the possibility of the supernatural and became an influential voice during the "New Age Movement" of the 1980s. See Vishal Mangalwadi. *This Book Changed Everything.* (Pasadena: SoughtAfterMedia, 2019), 34-36.

that it was their right to act upon evil thoughts (e.g., serial killers like Dennis Rader, a.k.a. "BTK"), while others, such as the Russian Ripper of Rostov, seemingly couldn't help themselves and pleaded to be killed by authorities once caught. In recent years there have been many killings that perpetrators blamed on demonic influences.[22]

Though drugs, mental disorders, or a combination of the two may cause people to do "evil" things, the evil people I am describing demonstrate lucid, rational thoughts, usually act with civility, and are completely sober.[23] Sociologists and psychologists can theorize and offer naturalistic explanations, but there are certain manifestations of evil in the world that cannot be explained outside of a religious context. Following decades of clinical assessment, Harvard-educated psychiatrist and best-selling author Scott Peck stated, "Evil human beings are quite common and usually appear quite ordinary to the superficial observer."[24] British philosopher, Roger Scruton, concurs with Peck and describes the difference between bad and evil people in the following manner:

> We distinguish people who are evil from those who are merely bad. Bad people are like you and me, only worse. They belong to the community, even if they behave badly toward it. We can reason with them, improve them, come to terms with them, and, in the end, accept them…But there are evil people who are not like that, since they do not belong in the community, even residing within its territory. Their bad behavior may be too secret and subversive to be noticeable, and any dialogue with them will be, on their part, a pretense. There is, in them, no scope for improvement, no path

[22] The Parkland School shooter Nikolas Cruz blamed a demon in his head for his actions. https://nypost.com/2018/08/07/parkland-shooter-blamed-demons-in-his-head-for-school-massacre/

[23] Katherine Ramsland. *Confession of a Serial Killer: The Untold Story of Dennis Rader, the BTK Killer.* (Hanover: ForEdge, 2017).

[24] M. Scott Peck. *People of the Lie: The Hope for Healing Human Evil.* (New York: Simon & Schuster, 1998, 47.)

to acceptance, and even if we think of them as human, their faults are not of the normal, remediable human variety but have another and more metaphysical origin. They are visitors from another sphere, incarnations of the Devil. Even their charm—and it is a recognized fact that evil people are often charming—is only further proof of their Otherness. They are, in some sense, the negation of humanity, wholly and unnaturally at ease with the thing that they seek to destroy....Whereas the bad person is guided by self-interest, to the point of ignoring or overriding the others who stand in his or her path, the evil person is profoundly interested in others, has almost selfless designs on them. The aim is not to use them.....but to rob them of themselves....We should not be surprised to find, therefore, that evil people are often opaque to us. However lucid their thoughts, however transparent their deeds, their motives are somehow uncanny, inexplicable, even supernatural.[25]

The adjectives used by Scruton to describe the demonic (charming, secretive, subversive, determined, calculated, uncanny, and influenced by otherworldly forces) are strikingly similar to adjectives used to describe the devil found both in scripture and the history of the church: attractive, beautiful, intelligent, crafty, uniquely strong-willed, maliciously intentional, deceptive, and dangerous (Gen. 3:1; Luke 22:31).

Those who have witnessed such perplexing behavior often don't know how to respond to it. I've heard several people struggle to find terminology that describes the enigmatic, evil behavior demonstrated by people they would never assume could be capable of it. It was as though someone they had known to be pleasant and good had been turned into, at least temporarily, something evil. Abnormal speech, the ability to speak in foreign languages a person had not studied, unrecognizable facial contortions, superhuman strength,

---

[25] Roger Scruton. *On Human Nature*. (Princeton: Princeton University Press, 2017, 134-135.)

uncontrollable rage in reaction to religious objects, or the sudden, inexplicable desire for the harm of self or others, are but some of the symptoms observed. Instead of trying to psychoanalyze or come up with an improbable explanation for people whose very essence, demeanor, and actions point to the demonic, why not call it what it is?

Recent national surveys have shown that roughly half of American adults believe in the devil and demons.[26] To this day, the Catholic Church actually trains priests to exorcise demons from those who are possessed, and the need for such training has increased in many parts of the world in response to pastoral demand.[27] It has been reported that in Italy alone more than 500,000 people visit an exorcist each year.[28] In the Catholic Rite of Baptism, those being baptized (or their godparents) promise to "renounce Satan, and all his works, and all his empty promises."[29] Though some may have a hard time understanding or believing that these encounters or practices have any real need or merit, there are many ministers, psychiatrists, and lay people who cannot deny a form of supernatural evil that they have observed to be real, thus justifying the need for the continued acknowledgement and renunciation of Satan.[30]

---

[26] The Baylor Institute for Studies of Religion Survey (2005, 2007); Portraits of American Life Study (2006).

[27] A friend living in Indiana witnessed evil physical manifestations within a neighbor and decided to turn to a local diocese for help. Evidently the one expert, a Catholic priest who is trained to perform exorcisms in that area, visits with nearly 300 people a year who are either severely oppressed or possessed by the demonic. https://www.telegraph.co.uk/news/2016/09/26/leading-us-exorcists-explain-huge-increase-in-demand-for-the-rit/ See also Matt Baglio. *The Rite: The Making of a Modern Exorcist.* (New York: Double Day, 2009).

[28] Baglio, 6.

[29] Fr. Mike Driscoll. *Demons, Deliverance and Discernment: Separating Fact from Fiction About the Spirit World.* (El Cajon, California: Catholic Answers, 2015), 14. Anglicans also use this or a similar form of words.

[30] Scott M. Peck. *Glimpses of the Devil: A Psychiatrist's Personal Accounts of Possession, Exorcisms and Redemption.* (New York: Free Press, 2005). Malachi Martin. *Hostage to the Devil: The Possession and Exorcism of Five Contemporary Americans.* (New York: Harper One, 1999).

The Undeniable d-EVIL

For those who struggle believing that invisible spiritual forces can influence our material world, discussing demonic influences seems strange, illogical, and unimaginable. Therefore, the mainstream media avoids explanations that are otherworldly, theological, or suggest that a supernatural realm exists. Even though the reality and consequences of supernatural activity seem hard for most people to deny, some choose to ignore it or always provide natural explanations. At the end of the day, denying the supernatural or the countless stories of its existence does not make it go away.

Believing in a devil has helped many people make sense of the world and the evil that has always been a part of it. It can be easy for one to dismiss the notion of God or a devil but much harder to deny the existence of evil. One merely has to observe the news headlines on any given day to be reminded of the evil that permeates the world. The problem of evil exists, and few deny it, but the differences lie in how people define, describe, explain, and deal with it. Skeptics often ask, "How can an all-powerful, loving God allow evil to exist?" It is a fair question that has led many people to deny the existence of God. However, when one considers the idea of the demonic as a viable option for explaining evil, things can start to make more sense. This thought led William Abraham from atheism to belief in God. Professor Abraham explains:

> If human agents are nothing more than complex configurations of physics and chemistry, then the whole idea of holding them accountable for evil melts into thin air. If our actions are physically determined, then it is simply incoherent to say that we are good or bad; we simply are what we are—complex, malfunctioning physical mechanisms, and that is the end of the matter. However, the problem of evil cuts deeper than even that for me. I sensed that to leave evil as a purely human phenomena was superficial. Perhaps there

is more than meets the eye in evil, I thought. In time I found that the idea of the demonic was entirely coherent. I had no firm idea what this might mean; but at the very least it meant that beyond human agents there lay the possibility of demonic agents who were hideously evil and who lured human agents into evil. Once I realized that the idea of the demonic was a coherent notion, my atheism began to crumble. If I could believe in the demonic as a possibility, then I could believe in God as a possibility, and my journey into atheism was immediately halted to a thud.[31]

Acknowledging the demonic is biblical, and it addresses the problem of evil head on. Rather than denying that God exists based on the existence of evil in the world, once one realizes that the inception of evil, and its continuation and consequences, are often tied to the demonic, one can find peace in the fact that Jesus came to defeat Satan, evil, sin, and death.

The Cosmic Battle

Before the creation of the world, a cosmic battle was going on behind the scenes, and occasionally humans catch sight of it. If you and I were provided a true glimpse of the actual war taking place in the spiritual realm, we might have trouble sleeping at night. This doesn't have to be the case, but it comes down to developing a proper understanding of the invisible battle. Theologian Peter Kreeft sums up well the two mistakes that people often make regarding the devil:

> Satan is equally pleased by our overestimating him *and* our underestimating him—as the commander of an enemy army in wartime would be equally pleased if your side greatly overestimated his strength and shook with superstitious fear when there was "nothing to fear but fear itself," or if you greatly underestimated his strength,

---

[31] Ibid, 165-166.

or even stopped believing in his very existence. Either mistake will certainly lose battles and possibly lose the war. If our ancestors tended to the mistake of overemphasizing the devil (and this was indeed unhealthy), we tend to the opposite mistake: forgetting that life is spiritual warfare, and that there is an enemy.[32]

Next to one's inherited sinful nature, the greatest and most challenging obstacle to each person's faith is a spiritual being known as the devil, originally called *Lucifer*. Given that the name *Lucifer* literally means "light bearer," it would seem unlikely that most people will ever see the scary version of the demonic found in many Hollywood movies or television shows. The devil is craftier than that, and he knows it will be much easier to defeat his opponents when they are oblivious to his presence. The deception seems to be working, for many people readily admit their belief in some type of god or higher power, yet still choose to dismiss the idea of a devil, or any really evil force, residing within a spiritual realm that can influence our physical world. Maybe the doubters are uncertain about whether or not evil spiritual forces actually exist, or perhaps wish to avoid being labeled as backwoods, unintelligent or delusional. This mentality has crept into the church as well, for some Christians live as though the devil does not exist, and if he does exist, they certainly don't want to talk about it.

The Biblical Devil

If you believe the Bible, then you really have no choice but to believe in the devil, for the Bible talks much about the devil and his army of demons. Jesus makes reference to the devil at least twenty-five times. Those who do not believe in a literal devil often argue that parts of the Bible should only be taken metaphorically. The Bible is

[32] Peter Kreeft. *Angels and Demons: What Do We Really Know About Them?* (San Francisco: Ignatius, 1995), 112-113. https://www.foxnews.com/science/root-of-humanitys-belief-in-evil-possibly-found

the surest guide to understanding the demonic world, and when it speaks of the devil, listen up. Pastor Chip Ingram warns:

> When scripture speaks of Satan, it isn't confined to small, passing comments or figures of speech. Satan is not a metaphor for evil. He is a powerful angel who committed treason against his Creator and convinced a third of the angels to rebel along with him. He now seeks to destroy all that is good and God-ordained, and his strategy ever since the fall has been to tempt us with the same agenda—to be like God.[33]

The Bible reveals that God created everything, including humans and all other creatures. Lucifer was the most beautiful and majestic of the angels and was given authority over the angelic world (Ezek. 28:14; Job 1:6; Col. 1:16). Though originally created good, because of envy and pride, Lucifer freely chose to disobey God and sin (Isa. 14:13; 1 Tim. 3:6; Jude 6). It has been said that pride comes before a fall, and this is exactly why Lucifer fell. There are two major passages from the Old Testament that most biblical scholars reference in relation to the "fall" of Satan (Ezek. 28:11-19 and Isa. 14:12-19). Like many parts of scripture, these passages point to dual realities—the fall of the king of Tyre in Ezekiel, and the king of Babylon in Isaiah—and both of those historical figures can serve as windows into the true spiritual forces behind them.[34]

Though we don't know exactly when Lucifer and one-third of the angels fell, we do know that it happened, for Jesus said, "I saw Satan fall like lightning from heaven" (Luke 10:18). We also know that the fall of Satan and the demons took place before the fall of Adam and Eve in the Garden of Eden. Satan enticed the first humans with the very thing that caused him to sin—to live independently of God by

---

[33] Chip Ingram. *The Invisible War: What Every Believer Needs to Know About Satan, Demons & Spiritual Warfare.* (Grand Rapids: Baker Books, 2015), 51-52.

[34] Ibid., 51.

disobeying God's law. Their disobedience is often referred to as "the Fall," or "original sin." It seems likely that the serpent appeared not as a dangerous or repulsive looking snake as you and I might imagine, but as an attractive, intelligent being posing as a friend. It is important to notice that since the very beginning of humanity, the devil hasn't always appeared as something negative to avoid, which is precisely why so many people have succumbed to the deception of the Enemy.[35]

What the creature might have looked like pales in comparison to what was said. The first humans were given freedom to enjoy all of God's magnificent creation and were restricted from only one thing —to eat fruit from a tree in the midst of the garden (Genesis 3). Satan tempted Adam and Eve with the idea that eating something they were instructed by God not to eat could somehow make their lives better. The Enemy wanted them to consider what was being presented, and what might be gained by consuming it, more so than what negative consequences might result from their actions. Rather than abiding in God's words and provision, they chose to believe the serpent's lie.

Just as Satan whispered to Eve attractive words of deception, he will likely whisper similar words that he thinks you want to hear. He won't speak literally, but will appeal to your sinful cravings through circumstances. When Christians are not focused on God's words, the Enemy's words can appear more attractive. Have you considered why the first humans were close enough to the forbidden tree in the first place? It seems that many people stand too close to the fires of temptation, despite knowing they might get burned. It can be hard to resist the lies, especially ones that seem true and make us feel good about ourselves and circumstances. Satan's lies cater to our innermost sinful desire of wanting to be in control. Such lies always come with

---

[35] Eugene Peterson. *As Kingsfishers Catch Fire: A Conversation on the Ways of God Formed by the Words of God.* (Colorado Springs: Waterbrook, 2017), 231.

a cost, and, ironically, do not serve us, but rather enslave us. This is why when we are tempted, we must always consider not just what is being offered, but what we may stand to lose.[36]

Implications of the Fall

The implications of the Fall were immediate, starting with the Lord declaring that "there will be enmity between Satan and mankind" (Gen. 3:15). Evil and sin entered the human world, and the devil was behind it. Jealousy, pride, greed, envy, shame, disease, and spiritual death were soon to follow. What had been created good became tarnished and broken as a result of being misused, abused, and perverted by mankind. Idolatry, which begins when humans treat the Creation, or anything in it, as if it were God, has plagued mankind since the fall of our first parents in the Garden of Eden.[37]

It started when the devil questioned God's words and convinced the first humans that they could be like God by living independently of him. It continues to this day as people try to find their identity, purpose, and happiness in anything other than God. Scripture and history are full of examples of people living for themselves instead of God and often replacing God with idols. The first book of the Bible describes how people tried to build a city with a tower that reached to the heavens so that they "could make a name" for themselves (Gen. 11:1-7). People are still trying to make a name for themselves by building their reputations, resumes, careers, and bank accounts, instead of pursuing all things for the glory of God.

Each day we are influenced in a variety of ways. Our culture, through the public education system, politics, social media, or the

---

[36] I.D. E. Thomas. *A Puritan Golden Treasury*. (Carlisle, PN: Banner of Truth Trust, 2000), 293.

[37] Tom Wright. *Spiritual and Religious: The Gospel in An Age of Paganism*. (London: Hodder & Stoughton, 1992), 28.

entertainment industry, seeks to promote behaviors that contradict the teachings of the Bible. Whether these negative influences find their way into our lives through classes, books, commercials, video games, podcasts, television shows, songs, movies, websites, or other forms of social media, people need to pay careful attention to what is influencing their minds, hearts, and souls during the waking hours of each day (even during the sleeping hours for those who fall asleep with the television on or listening to music). Even the consumption of what may appear to be desirable, popular, and good can end up negatively influencing our thoughts and behavior.

Around Halloween time, my kids look forward to consuming a ridiculous amount of candy. Who doesn't like candy? As a parent, I can lighten up and allow my kids to have exactly what they desire, for such fun and indulgence takes place but once per year, but I also must be ready to deal with the potential consequences of their hyperactivity and subsequent fatigue, toothaches, illness, and stomach aches. A diet of pure candy rots more than your teeth. Similarly, it is not uncommon to hear about the proverbial "freshman 15" that occurs when college students load up on cheap junk food, as well as adult beverages, without much restriction or care. Regardless of the stage of life, people of all ages need to pay attention to the intellectual and spiritual food they consume on a daily basis, for overindulgence, even of good things, can lead to all sorts of problems.

The Temptation of Jesus

Everyone is tempted by something. It is quite interesting to think about how the devil not only had the audacity to tempt Jesus to sin, but that he tried using the scriptures in the process. When the devil showed up to tempt Jesus in the wilderness, his plan was to trick the Messiah into believing that he possessed all authority, knowledge, and power and

was entitled to give this to Jesus. It was the same lie that he used to bait
Adam and Eve in the Garden of Eden. Satan falsely claimed to have
all authority in heaven and on earth, and desired to convince Jesus he
could have it too. It is important to notice that each time Satan tempted
him, Jesus never questioned whether or not the devil had the power
to make good on the offer. Jesus knows that Satan has power, which
is exactly why in other parts of scripture the devil has been referred to
as the "Prince of this World" (John 12:31). Though powerful, Satan's
abilities are limited. In order to understand the devil's tactics, let's take
a look at the passage concerning the temptation of Jesus:

> Jesus, full of the Holy Spirit, left the Jordan and was led by the
> Spirit into the wilderness, where for forty days he was tempted by
> the devil. He ate nothing during those days, and at the end of them
> he was hungry. The devil said to him, "If you are the Son of God,
> tell this stone to become bread." Jesus answered, "It is written: 'Man
> shall not live on bread alone.' The devil led him up to a high place
> and showed him in an instant all the kingdoms of the world. And
> he said to him, "I will give you all their authority and splendor;
> it has been given to me, and I can give it to anyone I want to. If
> you worship me, it will all be yours." Jesus answered, "It is written:
> 'Worship the Lord your God and serve him only.' The devil led him
> to Jerusalem and had him stand on the highest point of the temple.
> "If you are the Son of God," he said, "throw yourself down from
> here. For it is written: "'He will command his angels concerning
> you to guard you carefully; they will lift you up in their hands, so
> that you will not strike your foot against a stone. Jesus answered,
> "It is said: 'Do not put the Lord your God to the test.' When the
> devil had finished all this tempting, he left him until an opportune
> time. (Luke 4:1-13)

First, notice that it was "the Spirit that led Jesus into the wilderness"
(v. 1). This means that God not only allowed his Son to experience
the temptation of the devil, but actually led Jesus to the place of

temptation. Though Jesus may have been led there to be strengthened, the Enemy understood it as a means for temptation. This is vital for all Christians to understand, for God knows exactly what we are experiencing and sometimes allows challenging situations to occur for reasons we may never know. God never causes temptation, but sometimes allows temptation by the devil to take place, ultimately for his purposes and glory. A similar situation is mentioned at the beginning of the Old Testament Book of Job when God permitted the devil to challenge the faith of Job, a man regarded as "blameless, upright, and one who shunned evil" (Job 1:1). God not only allowed Job to be tempted, but he made the suggestion, "Have you considered my servant Job?" There is a false assumption among some Christians that if one has enough faith and lives a holy life then he or she will be immune from temptation or exempt from evil. If righteous Job and sinless Jesus were tempted, then no one gets a pass. The awareness of both God and the devil usually becomes more obvious when one really strives to know and live for God.

The first tactic used by the tempter was to question the identity of Jesus by asking, "If you are the Son of God..." (v. 3). The devil repeats the statement in verse nine. How many times in life have you doubted your status as being a child of God, or felt like the Enemy asked you a similar question: "If you really are a Christian ... ," or "Do you really believe that God loves you and has forgiven your sins?" Because Satan questioned the identity of Jesus, you can be certain that he will question yours as well, not to mention trying to cause you to doubt God's Word, true existence, and identity. Some have asked, "If Jesus was God in the flesh, why did the devil bother tempting him in the first place, for wouldn't the "God-man" be able to resist temptation?" This is a great question. Jesus was God in the flesh, but the devil refused to give up. Satan may be intelligent, but he has always been prideful, frustrated, vindictive, and stubborn. It is the reason why he disobeyed God and fell into sin, and it is the reason why he tempted Jesus. Notice the delusional, false promise the devil made: "I will give you all their authority and splendor; it has been given to me, and I can give it to anyone I want to. If you worship me, it will all be yours." Because all authority in heaven and on earth ultimately resides in Jesus, the King of Kings, the devil had no real chance of convincing Jesus to believe his lies, but it did not stop him from trying.

Jesus once said of Satan, "He has no claim on me" (John 14:30). Jesus had no weak spot whereby Satan could gain entrance into his life. This is not true of us. It is certain that Satan will continue to tempt Christ's followers when they are most vulnerable, and ironically, the times of vulnerability may come at the height of one's "success." The devil continues to lure with fame, money, and power, just as he did Christ.

Thankfully, Jesus demonstrated the way in which Christians should respond to these temptations. For each of the devil's questions and accusations, Jesus responded with scripture.[38] The devil knew the scriptures, but Jesus understood them. Notice that the devil actually misquoted scripture to trick Jesus into believing a perversion of the truth (vs. 10).[39] Though Jesus would not be deceived, you and I are susceptible to believing false interpretations of the scriptures. The devil has had centuries of exposure to God's words, and he loves to cause doubt, confusion, division, and sin by twisting them. Notice the very last verse of this passage: "When the devil had finished all his tempting, he left him until an opportune time" (v. 13). This verse proves that the devil's pride prevents him from accepting defeat, and though he will go away, he is always looking for the next opportunity to deceive. You and I are going to face temptation,

---

[38] Each time Jesus was tempted he responded by quoting the Old Testament book of Deuteronomy.

[39] The devil quoted the verse "He (God) will command his angels concerning you to guard you carefully," to imply that Jesus could act foolishly and expect a positive outcome. Jesus knew better, and therefore corrected the devil's incorrect usage of scripture by stating, "It says: Do not put the Lord your God to the test."

and hopefully we will be able to respond to Satan's lies with the truth of scripture.

Entering the Battle

The devil hates the people and things of God (Ephesians 6:12). The more closely you walk with Christ, the more you will realize that the "Prince of this World" is trying to gain powerful footholds within individual lives, as well as various aspects of society—universities, governments, families, the entertainment industry, etc.—all with the intention of causing division and destruction. Hostility toward Christians is increasing at an alarming rate in many countries, and sometimes in places that were founded upon Judeo-Christian values.

Though few will encounter the devil himself, there is a legion of demons that seek to destroy faith, service, and witness for God. I've heard many people mention that they had never truly noticed the Enemy until they became serious about their pursuit of God. Keep in mind that it is not about us, but the Enemy's constant desire to thwart God and kingdom work from taking place. This is why some of the greatest moments for Christians are sometimes followed by something trying to steal their joy. The last thing in the world the devil wants is for Christians to be joyful and excited about living for God and sharing the Good News with others. Because the devil envies joy, it is almost certain that he will try to steal it when given the opportunity. I can assure you that the Enemy will find all sorts of ways to prevent you from putting God first in your life, for when Christians serve with thanksgiving and joy, the Enemy is reminded of what he would not do. Esteemed pastor Chuck Swindoll explained it this way:

> Satan hates when people put God above all. He absolutely despises the Son of God, so the discipline that exemplifies Him will be one

that the devil will do his best to undo. As soon as you put this book down, I can almost guarantee you'll be met with a decision. Weigh it carefully. Your adversary knows the power of the immediate and will try to convince you that procrastinating isn't really denying God. Don't believe it![40]

Demonic activity tends to be more prevalent in areas where fruitful ministry is taking place, which is the reason why those on the frontlines of the spiritual battlefield often face the greatest opposition. The devil himself attacked Jesus at the beginning of his earthly ministry, and it is also the reason why so many ministers and missionaries are attacked as they strive to combat the works of the "ruler of this world." (Matt. 4:1-11; Luke 4:1-13; 2 Cor. 4:4). It makes sense that Christians are the most targeted for attack, for they are proclaiming the name that makes demons tremble. The New Testament mentions that demons believe in Jesus, and they shudder at his name (James 2:19). They can't stand Jesus, and they can't stand his followers, especially those called to vocational ministry and positions of leadership and influence. The great nineteenth-century pastor Charles Spurgeon was exactly right when he stated that, "Upon the whole, no place is so assailed with temptation as the ministry. The enemy has a special eye upon you, and he will spare you no further than God restrains him."[41] This reality applies to all Christians, but attacks are often more noticeable to those in vocational ministry.

Because Christians are the body of Christ, they will inevitably gain the attention of the one who opposes God's people and plan, especially when faithfully pursuing their calling. Not only will Christ and others know us by our fruits (good works), but Satan will also notice. I cannot count the number of times I have had Christians share with me that

---

[40] Charles R. Swindoll. *So, You Want to Be Like Christ? Eight Essentials to Get You There.* (Nashville: W Publishing Group, 2005), 186.

[41] Charles Spurgeon. *Lectures to My Students.* (Grand Rapids: Zondervan, 1954), 15-16.

an increase in the Enemy's opposition coincided with the Lord allowing them to experience success in ministry. Sometimes the opposition
happened just prior to the Lord using them to accomplish kingdom
work, and at other times the Enemy arrived to distract and disrupt a
fruitful ministry. Either way, as you strive to live for the glory and honor
of God, you should be prepared to face spiritual opposition. Once you
become a threat to the Enemy, the tension often becomes more obvious.

The Lord's brother, James, as well as the Apostle Peter, reminded
their audiences that they would face opposition for serving the Lord
(James 1:2-4; 1 Pet. 4:1). If you doubt this, sincerely begin to pray, read
the Bible and get to know Jesus, and you will likely also notice various
forms of distraction and opposition. So what might those attacks look
like?

The Accuser

One of the chief means by which the adversary attacks is condemning us for past sins. This can and does happen to Christians
regardless of their level of spiritual maturity. The devil often dredges
up past guilt that God has forgiven and no longer holds against us,
and then seeks to convince us that somehow the death of Christ on
the cross was insufficient to conquer our personal sins.[42] Don't believe
the lie! Don't let the Accuser rob you of the forgiveness, peace, and joy
that Christ's death and resurrection accomplished. Because there are
times when the Spirit of God brings conviction about unconfessed
sins, some have rightly asked, "How do I know the difference between
God convicting me of my sin, and the devil using past guilt and shame
to accuse me of something I have already confessed?" The answer is
that the conviction of God will drive us to humility, repentance, and

---

[42] R.C. Sproul. *Renewing Your Mind: Basic Christian Beliefs You Need to Know.* (Grand Rapids, Baker
Books, 1998), 201.

prayer, whereas the devil's accusations always lead to fear, worry, and despair.[43] Jesus declared, "In this world you will have trouble. But take heart! I have overcome the world" (John 16:33).

There is always a reason to rejoice, even amid the challenges, for as a Christian, you have been chosen and counted worthy to know, represent, and serve the King of Kings. The New Testament is filled with examples of believers who served with joy, despite being heavily persecuted (Ps. 94:19; Col. 1:12; Heb. 10:34; James 1:2; 1 Pet. 1:8). The best part about being a Christian is that Christ is always with us in spirit, and the Spirit gives us power (Matt. 28:18; 2 Tim. 1:7). As you learn to rely on God's strength, you will experience inexplicable peace and joy, even amid the trappings of the world and attacks of the Enemy.

Demon Possession

Scripture establishes that all Christians face demonic opposition at various times in life, and that the opposition is often more noticeable to those on the frontlines of the spiritual battle, but what are we to make of demonic possession? Because of several popular movies that have portrayed people being possessed by demons, some have asked the question, "Can a Christian be demon-possessed?" It seems unlikely, for the Bible does not provide a single example of a Christian being possessed by a demon. It is one thing to be tempted, pestered, discouraged, influenced, or persuaded by the demonic, and quite another to actually be possessed.

Clearly, demonic possessions took place during biblical times, as recorded in the scriptures (Mark 1:21-28, 5:1-20, 9:14-29). It has been said that 25 percent of Jesus's ministry had to do with deliverance from

---

[43] Ibid.

demonic possession (Matt. 8:16; Mark 1:32-34; Luke 6:18).[44] Aside from one instance in which Jesus laid hands upon the possessed person, the demons would flee either when they saw him coming, or as soon as he commanded them to leave (Luke 13:10-13; Matt. 6:18, Mark 9:20; Luke 8:28). The Bible does speak about Christians being *oppressed* by demons, but there is no biblical evidence of a Christian being possessed by a demon (Eph. 6:10-14, 1 Pet. 5:8).

It seems unlikely that one who has the indwelling Holy Spirit could be simultaneously possessed by a demon, even though some have claimed otherwise.[45] The Bible refers to the Christian as a temple of the Holy Spirit (1 Cor. 6:19). Is it logical for a temple to have two diametrically opposed rulers? People may interpret the word *"possession"* in different ways, and therefore sincerely make the argument that a Christian may have experienced things that were symptomatic of New Testament demonic activity; such claims, however, can never receive explicit biblical endorsement because there are no biblical examples of a Christian being possessed by a demon.[46] On extremely rare occasions when actual demonic possession has taken place, instances were usually preceded by one actively seeking a pathway to the demonic or resulting from generational involvement with the demonic world.[47]

---

[44] Ingram, 186.

[45] https://www.theamericanconversative.com/dreher/devils-of-manhattan/

[46] John L. Gillhooly. *40 Questions About Angels, Demons, and Spiritual Warfare.* (Grand Rapids: Kregel, 2018), 79. Gilhooly correctly points out that, "arguments from experience are not self-interpreting, no matter how sincere, but need to be interpreted in light of what Scripture claims." See also M. Scott Peck. *People of the Lie: The Hope for Healing Human Evil.* (New York: Simon & Schuster, 1998).

[47] Ibid, 190-198. Ingram mentions that the pathways to demonic influences are sin, spiritual rebellion, and active seeking (via occult activities, such as witchcraft, Ouija boards, mediums, etc.). Ingram also provides symptoms that accompanied some of the demonic examples found in New Testament: severe sickness (Matt. 12:22), divination (Acts 16:16), unusual physical strength (Mark 5:2-3), fits of rage (Mark 5:4), split personality (Mark 5:6-7), resistance to spiritual help (Mark 5:7), other voices within (Mark 5:9), and occult powers (Deut. 18:10-11).

Knowing Your Enemy

We need to know our enemy, understand his nature, abilities, and agenda. Satan is a created, finite being, which means that he is limited in power and inferior to his Creator. Though he has been referred to as the "Prince of this World," the "Prince of Demons," the "God of this Age," and "the ruler of the kingdom of the air," his power is subject to God's permission, and he can only operate within the boundaries set by the sovereign Lord (Matt. 12:24; John 12:31; 2 Cor. 4:4; Eph. 2:2; Job 1:6-12). He has always been envious of God, and his pride led to his rebellion and subsequent "fall" (Isa. 14:13; 1 Tim. 3:6). Christ is the "Holy One," whereas Satan is called the "Evil One" (John 17:15; Rev. 16:5). Satan is a counterfeit who is constantly trying to imitate the only true God (Isa. 14:13). This is the reason why the devil has been referred to as a roaring lion, for he so desperately wants to rule like Christ, who is the Lion of the tribe of Judah and true King of Creation (1 Peter 5:8; Revelation 5:5, 9:16). Despite the Enemy's insatiable desire to be like God, there really is no comparison. Christ decreed the end from the beginning, created time and is outside of it, whereas Satan's time is limited (Rev. 22:13).

Unlike God, the devil is not omnipresent. Though Satan cannot be in more than one place at a time, he can and does send his subordinate demonic agents to entice Christians and non-Christians alike, to sin (Eph. 6:12). Jesus is "the way, the truth, and the life" (John 14:6), whereas Satan is the "Father of Lies" (John 8:44). Jesus came so that we might have life, and have it to the full, whereas Satan was a murderer from the beginning and seeks to steal, kill, and destroy (Matt. 8:22; John 10:10).

Satan is more powerful than any human, but that power is limited, and therefore wholly in subjection to God's unlimited power.[48] Though Satan is more intelligent than any human being, he is not omniscient, and he is ignorant in comparison to the One who knows everything. Satan wants to be worshiped and adored as the one who rules the world, but Almighty God reigns supreme, and is the only one worthy of the praise of every creature. Satan and demons do the tempting, and God always provides a way to escape, or the ability to withstand (1 Cor. 10:13). God does what is best for his children, whereas Satan, which literally means "adversary," is fully committed to their misery and demise. Christ brings unity, while Satan causes division. Another word for devil, *diabolus*, literally means "throwing apart."

Though Satan attempts to control the world, the entire world is in the hands of the sovereign Creator and Sustainer of it. While Satan attempts to cause confusion and fear, God promises peace that is beyond understanding (Isa. 26:3). The ultimate aim of the tempter is to cause failure, whereas God wants us to resist the temptation and become stronger. Satan wants people to find their value in the things of this world, whereas Christ urges us to store our treasures in heaven (Matt. 6:19-20). Satan wants people to feel inadequacy, shame, and despair, but when Christ becomes their ultimate treasure, they feel forgiven, hopeful, and empowered. While Satan bribes us with temporary pleasures that fade away, Christ promises everlasting joy for those who seek first his kingdom and righteousness (Matt. 6:33). Instead of chasing Satan's fleeting bribes and empty lies, those who find their value in Christ will experience the abundant life now and one day will receive his promise of an eternal inheritance.

---

[48] It has been said that Satan is God's devil, and that he is kept on a short, tight leash, which means that he cannot do anything without God's knowledge and permission (Job 1:12). This might not seem comforting to someone going through a difficult time, but can serve as a reminder to trust the character of God even when one cannot make sense of what God has allowed.

Temptation and You

Temptation is part of every person's life because each of us is born with a sinful nature. It will never go away. Even atheists must admit that there are "temptations" out there which bring nothing but deceit and destruction. Temptation does not discriminate, and it is no respecter of persons. Religious or irreligious, everyone is tempted by something, and at times most of us actually like it. Why else do we browse online and shop at our favorite stores looking for things that we don't really need and sometimes can't afford? Sometimes temptation is obvious, but oftentimes we are not aware of it. The tempter is observant and aware of our desires. He is also patient and seeking the opportune time to attack when we are most likely to succumb. Though the devil and demons can deceive and tempt people to sin, they do not cause people to sin. Demonic forces often make appeals to the innate, sinful cravings of humans, similar to a fisherman enticing his catch with specific bait. The New Testament writer James describes the process:

> Let no one say when he is tempted, 'I am being tempted by God,' for God cannot be tempted with evil, and he himself tempts no one. But each person is tempted when he is lured and enticed by his own desire (sinful nature). Then desire when it has conceived gives birth to sin. (James 1:13-15)

Sin is passive indifference to God, as well as an active rebellion against God.[49] It is not just about doing bad things, but choosing to make the good of God's creation more important than God.[50]

Because Christianity is a spiritual battle full of daily temptations, it is really important to be aware of how temptation works in your

[49] Mike Strauss. *The Creator Revealed: A Physicist Examines the Big Bang Theory and the Bible.* (Bloomington, IN: Westbrow Press, 2018), 125.
[50] Tim Keller, *The Reason for God,* 168.

own life. What might be tempting to one person might not appeal to another person. Depending on your stage in life, temptation may come through a new or desired relationship, pursuit of a particular college, degree, job, career, promotion, social status, or various forms of monetary gains. Success in the eyes of the world seems to justify the sins of many. Too often people engage in things that are borderline unethical as long as their actions are legal, popular, or lead to wealth or power. Sometimes good things can end up being exploited by dark forces resulting in negative consequences. Any good thing can become an idol. A job promotion is usually a very good thing, yet if it leads to someone neglecting more important priorities, such as God, family, and friends, it can end up being more of a curse than a blessing. Being part of a club, fraternity, or sorority during college can provide acceptance, friendship, and a lot of fun, but it may also be the thing that causes one's grades, or health, both physical and spiritual, to suffer.

Because of my love for sports, I tend to watch ESPN for about thirty minutes per day. It's enjoyable, fits into my schedule, and is no big deal on most days. However, if I decide to watch ESPN for six hours one day instead of taking my kids to school or going to work, I'm going to have to deal with the negative consequences. In this current generation, statistics show that the average person devotes nearly six hours per day engaged in some form of digital media, whether it be a smartphone, computer screen, or other electronic device.[51]

So much of life has to do with finding balance. Perhaps you've heard the expression, "the devil is in the details." I've found that he can be in every detail of life that is not fully committed to God—relationships, school, job, sports, hobbies, and whatever else you may be

---

[51] https://www.pcmag.com/news/tech-addiction-by-the-numbers-how-much-time-we-spend-online

involved in. Most of us are busier than we'd like to be, and it is usually of our own making. Some claim to be multi-tasking in order to save time and work more efficiently, even though they may be on the verge of becoming a workaholic. I've known many men who started out as great husbands and dads but allowed an overly busy work schedule to take priority over everything else, including their family. It can happen to anyone, at any age and at any time.

Regardless of your stage in life, be careful not to let busyness rob the time and energy needed for people and things that should matter most in your life, especially God. Busyness is often a symptom of a bigger problem, which is usually the pursuit of acceptance, money, power, or fame. For a high school or college student, being involved in too many extracurricular activities, or trying to live for the approval of others, can lead to exhaustion and despair. Everyone will be tempted by something. Even one's family or ministry can become an idol! So be alert, and learn to be intentional, and even selfish, about your time with God. Guard it! Put the meeting with God on your calendar if you must. It is not about checking off boxes. It is about knowing and becoming more like Christ, and allowing that relationship to guide all other relationships and aspects of your life. We should seek the face of God each morning (*coram deo*) before seeking the face of anyone else. If you don't make God the first priority in your daily life, you will always struggle to find true peace and joy that can come only through knowing and living for Christ (Matt. 6:33).

Some Christians live as if the devil doesn't exist, and if Christ and the Bible have no authority. Most people know right from wrong but are willing to take their chances and ignore the potential consequences of making poor decisions. Sometimes college students chose to ignore Christianity simply because they would rather live in sin and embrace their newfound freedom. One's career can also introduce a variety of distractions. Regardless of our stage in life, God has provided both advice and warnings in the scriptures, and we need to listen. It is important to take advantage of the wisdom provided by the Bible, and by the people who are looking out for our best interests. Even if the warnings don't make sense, seem boring, or might keep us from doing something that we think is fun or seemingly harmless, ignoring them can harm friendships, marriages, careers, and good reputations. The short-term gain of sin can have long-term consequences.

At times there will be a chink in every person's spiritual armor that allows the Enemy an open shot. Oftentimes the most challenging temptations occur when one is desperate, vulnerable, alone, tired, angry, discouraged, or lacking accountability. However, temptations may also come while being surrounded by many people, perhaps at a club, bar, concert, or other social event where people try to blend in, remain anonymous, and enjoy what everyone else is doing. It has been said that misery loves company, and a crowd can temporarily lessen one's guilt, numb pain, provide a false sense of acceptance or purpose, and also deceive one into thinking that what seems popular must not be that bad. As a Christian, you may appear spiritually strong to those around you, but always realize that your weaknesses are not hidden from the devil. The Apostle Paul warned the Christians in Corinth against overconfidence in their ability to resist temptation. It would be wise for everyone to heed his warning:

> So, if you think you are standing firm, be careful that you don't fall! No temptation has seized you except what is common to man. And God is faithful; he will not let you be tempted beyond what you can bear. But when you are tempted, he will also provide a way out so that you can stand up under it. (1 Corinthians 10:12-13)

Roaring Lion or Angel of Light?

It is much harder to avoid danger when you are not aware of it. The Apostle Paul was very explicit in his warning to the Christians living in Ephesus about the Enemy's overarching involvement in the spiritual battle, stating, "We do not wrestle against flesh and blood, but against the rulers, against the authorities, against cosmic powers over this present darkness, against spiritual forces of evil in the heavenly places" (Eph. 6:12). The Apostle Peter likened the devil's ferocious intentions to that of "a roaring lion looking for someone to devour" (1 Pet. 5:8). The imagery used to describe the devil in the New Testament emerged at a time when Christians were suffering severe persecution, both from Jewish authorities and Roman rulers, and the biblical authors wanted to remind their readers that evil spiritual forces were influencing much of it.

Most people living in developing countries today, especially missionaries, know that supernatural evil exists without needing convincing. For some people, the world around them is so spiritually dark and hopeless that they cannot ignore the roar of the vicious "lion" that seeks to take advantage of its victims through various forms of abuse and manipulation (e.g., human sex trafficking, slavery, false ideologies, theft, and terrorism). Many westerners, on the other hand, fail to realize the extent of the Enemy's deception because the devil has often disguised himself as "an attractive angel of light" (2 Cor. 11:14). It is quite interesting to juxtapose the Apostle Paul's "angel of light" description with the Apostle Peter's "roaring lion" imagery. Naturally, one may ask, "Which description of the devil is most accurate?" It seems that the Enemy will adapt to each person's circumstances in order to cause the most harm and confusion. It also seems that in many non-western contexts the "roaring lion" scares people into the occult and all sorts of desperate measures to find peace and ward off evil. Oftentimes the victims are simply trying to survive.

In most western contexts, however, the devil appears as an "angel of light" to conceal his true identity and intentions. For many Europeans and Americans, the idea and awareness of a spiritual realm, much less spiritual danger, is usually ignored because the Enemy has disguised himself so well. People seldom notice the deception because the Deceiver avoids any manifestation that might resemble a weird, grotesque, or exaggerated depiction found in a Hollywood movie. Theologian Warren Smith correctly points out that, "It is precisely because evil is camouflaged with the appearance of goodness that it is hard to tell the difference between what is truly good and what is corrupted goodness. This is the source of evil's deceptive power. This is what makes the temptation so seductive."[52] Because the devil is a creature, he has no ability to create anything. Rather, he takes all that is good with God's creation and distorts, perverts, twists, confuses, misuses, and exploits. He also uses the good to tempt people to do evil. Because the temptations are often subtle and cloaked in virtues, many fail to see the danger coming. The bottom line is that every generation of Christians has struggled with trying to distinguish good from evil. The Apostle John provided the earliest Christians with advice that is just as relevant today:

> Dear friends, do not believe every spirit, but test the spirits to see whether they are from God, because many false prophets have gone out into the world. This is how you can recognize the Spirit of God: Every spirit that acknowledges that Jesus Christ has come in the flesh is from God, but every spirit that does not acknowledge Jesus is not from God. This is the spirit of the antichrist, which you have heard is coming and even now is already in the world. (1 John 4:1-4)

---

[52] J. Warren Smith. *The Lord's Prayer: Confessing the New Covenant.* (Eugene, Oregon: Cascade Books, 2015), 121.

This means that even some of the seemingly supernatural things that take place, though miraculous, may not be of God. Sorcery, magic, and the like were prevalent during biblical times, and still occupy some portions of modern culture as well. The Bible mentions that demons can deceive people through "counterfeit miracles, signs and wonders" (2 Thess. 2:9). Most people who are aware of danger and deception will usually avoid it, but the ones who are not, could end up being distracted, misled, deceived, or harmed because of their ignorance. Most will not intentionally dabble in what historically has been tied to the occult or demonic world, but everyone is susceptible to common forms of deception that can influence aspects of everyday life (pride, greed, lust, envy, etc.). Sometimes even good things can end up being exploited by dark forces to result in negative consequences, which is why praying for discernment, knowing the scriptures, and seeking wise counsel should play a prominent role in one's daily life.

The Father of Lies

The devil is constantly distorting truth, which is why Jesus referred to him as the "Father of Lies" (John 8:44). The most dangerous and convincing lies are the ones that sound believable because they contain kernels of truth. Because the Bible contains the inspired words of God, and is therefore the ultimate source of truth, it will always be twisted and under attack. In the Garden of Eden, the serpent attacked God's words and planted seeds of doubt by asking the first humans, "Did God really say….?" (Genesis 3:3). There were numerous times in college when I heard skeptical professors ask similar questions with the intention of undermining God's words. I'm not suggesting that people who are skeptical about the Bible are being guided by Satan, but I have no doubt that the questions and criticisms leveled against Christians and the Bible can be exploited by the Enemy to cause doubt and confusion.

Learn to welcome the questions and challenges, because finding God's answer will strengthen you. Sometimes the questions raised are valid and should not be easily dismissed, but keep in mind that an enemy exists who would love nothing more than for you to doubt the veracity of the Bible. This is why having a strong grasp of the scriptures is so important, for along the way you will be tempted to believe false interpretations of it.

I have known quite a few people who grew up in the church only to end up walking away from the faith as a result of hearing false interpretations of the Bible. People who do not know what scripture says can be easily mislead by skeptics who have actually read the Bible. This is the reason why so many teenagers and college students experience a crisis of faith when someone starts asking questions, making fun of, or critiquing the Bible that Christians supposedly hold so dear, yet know so little about. The sad reality is that many Christian parents and leaders do not expect their children and students to read and know the Bible, and part of the reason is because no one ever challenged them to make it a priority in their lives. Because many churches are not teaching people how to study the Bible for themselves, charlatans have misled gullible Christians for years, and many have done so in the name of Christ through false teaching and misuse of the scriptures. Such irresponsible leadership causes people to believe false promises that are not found in the Bible, and eventually can make it easier for them to disregard their unrealistic versions of Christianity and the Bible that were based on lies and shallow preaching.[53]

---

[53] The "Prosperity Gospel," or "Health-Wealth Gospel," has been documented and explained well in Kate Bowler's seminal book, *Blessed: A History of the American Prosperity Gospel.* (New York: Oxford University Press, 2013). Basically, if one has strong faith, prays, and gives enough money to their respective church, "health and wealth" are bound to follow. Given that so many Christ followers, recorded both in scripture and the history of the church were poor, sometimes physically and monetarily, it is easy to see why many have adamantly opposed the "prosperity gospel."

Unfortunately, people who do not know the scriptures usually don't know God as they should, or the fact that they are being misled. Those who refuse to learn the scriptures are much more likely to be led astray by perversions of it, and the Father of Lies will continue to take full advantage of the opportunities to promote doubt and confusion. One who knows the truth more completely will be able to stand in its claims more fully, while simultaneously dismissing the half-truths that may present themselves.

Spiritual Resources

Finally, be strong in the Lord and in his mighty power. Put on the full armor of God, so that you can take your stand against the devil's schemes. For our struggle is not against flesh and blood, but against the rulers, against the authorities, against the powers of this dark world and against the spiritual forces of evil in the heavenly realms. Therefore, put on the full armor of God, so that when the day of evil comes, you may be able to stand your ground, and after you have done everything, to stand... And pray in the Spirit on all occasions with all kinds of prayers and requests. With this in mind, be alert and always keep on praying for all the Lord's people. (Eph. 6:10-13; 18)

God has provided every Christian with the knowledge, power, and ability to resist sinful impulses and the spiritual attacks of demonic forces. The Bible and prayer are chief among the spiritual resources that are readily available. Always remember that the "Word" of God, Jesus Christ, speaks in a variety of ways, including through the written words that we find in the Bible, but also through the words of preaching used by the apostles and evangelists, the words of our well-formed consciences, the words that the "heavens are declaring (Ps. 19), and so forth. Scripture is living, active, and more powerful than a two-edged sword, and it does not return void (Heb. 4:12; Isa.

55:11). In fact, even hell cannot prevail against the power of Christians who are proclaiming and living by the power of the Holy Spirit working through the scriptures (Matt. 16:18). This doesn't mean that knowing, or even memorizing scripture will always make life easier, but it will certainly help.

Because we live in a confused and distracted world, there are many things vying for our attention and allegiance that contradict Christianity and the Bible. If we are not worshipping God, we are essentially worshipping someone or something else (the pursuit of fame, popularity, status in the community, money, grades, the approval of others, etc.). Each day we must choose to follow Christ, who is the "Prince or Peace," or follow the devil, who is the "Prince of this World." In the Gospel of Matthew Jesus said, "No one can serve two masters, we will either hate the one and love the other, or we will be devoted to one and despise the other" (Matt. 6:24). Though the occasion regarded money, the principle is universally accepted. Satan wants to be your master, or as the band Metallica would say in reference to drugs controlling its victims, the "Master of Puppets."

The tempter will try to take control over the areas of your life that are least surrendered to God, whether it has to do with your identity, family, friendships, job, marriage, church, career, hobbies, or something else. Therefore, the more parts of your life that are surrendered to God, the more difficult it will be for the Enemy to gain control. He may use money, drugs, sex, pornography, gambling, social media, fantasy sports, and a plethora of other things to distract your mind and destroy your faith and witness. Unbelief, worry, and fear are at the top of the list of distractions for many people, but this doesn't have to be the case. Regardless of whether or not the distractions are from the world, of your own making, or result from the imposition or exploitation of the Enemy, the Apostle Paul provided instruction to the Christians living in Philippi that is just as applicable today:

> Do not to be anxious about anything, but in everything, by prayer and petition, with thanksgiving, to present our requests to God. And the peace of God, which transcends all understanding, will guard our hearts and minds in Christ Jesus. Finally, brothers, whatever is true, whatever is noble, whatever is right, whatever is pure, whatever is lovely, whatever is admirable—if anything is excellent or praise-worthy—think about these things. (Phil. 4:6-8)

Centuries earlier, the prophet Isaiah recorded a similar admonition: "the one whose mind is focused on me, declares the Lord, I will keep in perfect peace" (Isa. 26:3). We must learn to focus our minds on things above, the godly things, not the earthly, temporal distractions that are all around us.

The Bible reminds us that the whole world is under the power of the evil one, which means that without God's grace, protection and provision, we are defenseless and helpless against the supernatural power of the devil (1 John 5:19). This means that you and I are experiencing God's amazing grace, mercy, and restraint of evil forces every single day, whether we realize it or not. It is worth repeating the words of the Apostle Peter, who also warned Christians to be alert and watch out for the devil's tactics: "Be self-controlled and alert. Your enemy, the devil, prowls around like a roaring lion looking for someone to devour. Resist him, standing firm in the faith, because you know that your brothers throughout the world are undergoing the same kind of sufferings" (1 Pet. 5:8). Pastor Brian Hedges explains the importance of today's disciples being aware of and on guard against the devil's schemes:

> To watch, then, means to "watch out." To be aware. Your enemy is more unrelenting than a Black Rider hunting the Ring of Power (in the *Lord of the Rings*). He is more vicious than an angry cobra cornered by a mongoose. He never goes on vacation. Watch your

enemy because he is watching you.[54]

The Enemy is watching, and will attempt to overtake you in a place where you lie most vulnerable to his attacks.[55] When we pray, "Lead us not into temptation, but deliver us from evil," we are really asking God to grant us the ability to endure the temptations of the evil one (1 John 5:19). Because the attacks may come on those closest to you (parents, friends, children, etc.), it is important to cover them with the authority of Christ each day. This is one of the reasons why praying is so important, especially for discernment, wisdom, and strength.

This is also why we are to pray in Jesus's name. There is power in the name of Jesus, and demons flee when they hear his name being proclaimed, for it reminds them of their status as rebellious, defeated creatures. Therefore, if and when you sense the presence of the Enemy, pray for God's strength to empower you to overcome temptation, and proclaim the name of Jesus aloud for all to hear, for fear turns to power when the name of Jesus is proclaimed.

Conclusion

> There are two equal and opposite errors into which our race can fall about the devils. One is to disbelieve in their existence. The other is to believe, and to feel an excessive and unhealthy interest in them. C.S. Lewis -The Screwtape Letters, p. 3, preface

My parting advice is that you should spend your time focusing on the Lord, not thinking about the devil. The Enemy doesn't want you to think he exists, but once you realize that he does, different forms of distraction and deception are less likely to cause frustration,

---

[54] Brian G. Bridges. *Watchfulness: Recovering A Lost Spiritual Discipline.* (Grand Rapids: Reformation Heritage Books, 2018), 14.

[55] Charles Spurgeon. *Spurgeon on Prayer and Spiritual Warfare.* (New Kensington, PA: Whitaker House), 1998, 503.

confusion, discouragement, and fear. Angels and demons are real, even if you never notice their presence. There is no reason to deny them, nor develop some type of unhealthy obsession that can lead only to superstition, paranoia, or coming across as a nut case.

Always keep in mind that many of the negative things you experience in life may have more to do with your own poor choices than anything else. There will be times when you won't be able to tell the difference between something that resulted from your own sinful desires, the bad choices of others, or the direct influence of the demonic. Because faith, intellect, stamina, and toughness will never be enough, Christ must always be your ultimate strength and shield. There is no perfect battle plan to defeat the Enemy, despite prescriptions being offered by some television preachers. Even more importantly, the battle is not yours to begin with, and you could never win even if it were. The devil doesn't care about you. We are all jokes to him. He is ultimately out to get God, and we are merely caught up in the battle.

Your spiritual life should be more about focusing on and knowing Christ than trying to avoid temptation, sin, and the devil. Living a God-centered life enables one to live in victory instead of fear. Ultimately, it is not about what you can do, but about what Christ has done. Your identity must be rooted in Christ, for Jesus said, "I am the vine; you are the branches. If you remain in me, and I in you, you will bear much fruit; apart from me you can do nothing" (John 15:5). Therefore, whether you are a new Christian or one who has followed Jesus for decades, there are certain things that should be part of your daily life to help you draw closer God (there is a chapter about prayer near the end of the book).

The Bible states that if we draw near to God, he will draw near to us. When Christians obey this command, ultimately the devil will flee (James 4:7). This is easier said than done, especially when one becomes overwhelmed by the stresses of life. What matters most is striving to live for God by being like Christ, and not allowing anything to distract you from that pursuit. Scripture tells us that God is light, and, "If we walk in the light, as he is in the light, we have fellowship with one another, and the blood of Jesus, his Son, purifies us from all sin" (1 John 1:7). Jesus is the powerful light that exposes and expels the darkness. The words he inspired in the Bible are to be "a lamp unto our feet" (Psalm 119:105). This is why we should read, study, learn, and use the scriptures to light our path through the darkness of this world. Prayer should be about talking to the Lord, for it is the presence and love of Christ that we all so desperately need. Reflect on the Apostle Paul's reminder of this reality:

> For I am convinced that neither death nor life, neither angels nor demons, neither the present nor the future, nor any powers, neither height nor depth, nor anything else in all creation, will be able to separate us from the love of God that is in Christ Jesus our Lord. (Romans 8:38-39)

The battle is ultimately the Lord's, and Christians should live in the victory that Christ has already won through his death and resurrection. Tom Wright explains the victory of the cross:

> It was the victory of weakness over strength, the victory of love over hatred. It was the victory that consisted in Jesus allowing evil to do its worst to him, and never attempting to fight it on its own terms. When the power of evil had made its last possible move, Jesus had still not been beaten by it. He bore the weight of the world's evil to the end, and outlasted it.[56]

Though always a temporary threat, sin and the devil have ultimately been defeated (1 John 3:8). One should take the devil seriously,

---

[56] Tom Wright. *Spiritual and Religious: The Gospel in An Age of Paganism.* (London: Hodder & Stoughton, 1992), 66.

while always remaining confident in Christ. Recall the Apostle Paul's reminder to the Christians living in Colossae:

> Jesus forgave us all our sins, having canceled the written code, with its regulations, that was against us; he took it away, nailing it to the cross. And having disarmed the powers and authorities, he made a public spectacle of them, triumphing over them by the cross. (Colossians 2:13-15)

Christ's victory is our victory over sin, death, and the dark powers that occupy both the spiritual realm, and the world where we temporarily reside. When we seek first God's kingdom and righteousness above all else, he will provide the strength needed to flourish in the journey, no matter what schemes might be employed by the evil one (Matt. 6:33). When we depend on God's strength, utilize the protection and power of his Word, and approach his throne of grace with confidence and humility through prayer, we will be able to overcome the world, the flesh, and the devil!

Questions for Discussion:

1. Do you believe in the devil, angels, and demons? Why or why not?

2. Do you believe that your greatest enemy is a spiritual force? Why or why not?

3. Based on Matthew 4:1-11 and Luke 4:1-13, how did Jesus respond to the temptations of the devil? What do Christ's responses say about his authority? Could you respond in a similar way when tempted?

4. Temptation can result from sinful desires, enticements of the devil, or a combination of both. Regardless of the cause of the temptation, how should one respond to it?

5. Regarding temptations, why is it important for you to know your areas of weakness? Can you list your weaknesses? Can you see how an intelligent being could use the world's systems and your sinful nature to entrap you? How?

6. What are some things you can do to prevent and resist temptations and schemes of the devil?

7. Do you sense spiritual tension or opposition in your life? If not, what might this indicate about your spiritual life and what you are pursuing?

8. What does "putting on the armor of God" mean for Christians? How might that look in your life?

For Further Reading:

C.S. Lewis. *The Screwtape Letters.* New York: Harper Collins, 1942.

Chip Ingram. *The Invisible War: What Every Believer Needs to Know About Satan, Demons & Spiritual Warfare.* Grand Rapids: Baker Books, 2015.

Charles Spurgeon. *Spurgeon on Prayer and Spiritual Warfare.* New Kensington, PA: Whitaker House, 1998.

WHAT THE HELL?

The term *"hell"* has been part of the vernacular for centuries. In relation to sports you might hear someone exclaim, "That was a hell of a shot, a hell of a catch, a hell of a game, or a hell of a team!" I remember asking a friend about how he enjoyed a recent vacation, to which he replied, "It was a hell of a trip." In each of those cases the word hell was used to convey something surprisingly pleasant, unlikely or good.

"You can go to hell" is an expression that has been uttered by some angry people on occasion. I've heard people label a past occupation as being "the job from hell." Another common usage of the term occurs during the heat of the summer when some people exclaim, "It is hotter than hell today!" At some point you might hear someone ask, "What the hell just happened," or "What in the hell are you doing?" In each of these cases the term was used in reference to something negative. In relation to religion, seldom does the term invoke thoughts of peace, happiness or grandeur in the minds of most people.

For many people, even some Christians, the subject isn't truly considered until high school or college. Hell has been described as a very dreadful place in many works of literature over the centuries.

Twentieth-century atheist Jean-Paul Sartre's play *No Exit* declared that "hell is other people." Some people think of images from Dante's literary masterpiece, the *Inferno*. As the poet Dante approached the entrance to hell, he heard the screams and anguish of the damned souls that were rejected by God. He then looked up and read the inscription above the entrance:

BEFORE ME NOTHING BUT ETERNAL THINGS
WERE MADE, AND I SHALL LAST ETERNALLY.
ABANDON EVERY HOPE, ALL WHO ENTER[1]

Some envision hell to be a place where the devil is waiting to punish bad people as soon as they arrive. A few college students suggested to me that hell will be a party with their best friends, similar to their current lifestyle on earth, but much bigger.

The majority of people who believe in God also believe in hell. A recent survey spanning sixty-three countries revealed that 83 percent of Christian and Muslim adults believe in hell.[2] Studies have also shown that nearly 60 percent of all adults believe in some version of hell.[3] Despite widespread belief, rarely is hell a topic of conversation. It is a complicated and controversial subject to say the least. I agree with Peter Kreeft, who said, "Of all the doctrines of Christianity, hell is probably the most difficult to defend, the most burdensome to believe, and the first to be abandoned."[4] When the topic is broached, the reactions vary widely.

In 2007, outspoken atheist Christopher Hitchens was asked his opinion concerning the passing of prominent Christian leader, Jerry

[1] Dante Alighieri. *The Divine Comedy, Volume I: Inferno*. (New York: Penguin, 2003), 89.

[2] https://www.pewforum.org/2016/03/22/women-and-men-about-equally-likely-to-believe-in-heaven-hell-and-angels

[3] https://www.pewforum.org/religious-landscape-study/belief-in-hell/

[4] Peter Kreeft and Ronald Tacelli. *Handbook of Christian Apologetics: Hundreds of Answers to Crucial Questions*. (Downers Grove: IVP Academic, 1994,) 282.

Falwell. When the reporter asked Hitchens, "Do you believe in heaven, and if you do, do you believe that Jerry Falwell is in it?" Hitchens replied, "No, and I think it's a pity that there isn't a hell for him to go to." It was a damning statement indeed, yet that sentiment is held by some people who claim no religious affiliation, especially when they think about those who believe in a literal hell and actually want to talk about it. For some, it is much easier to dismiss it altogether, especially if their loved ones might end up there. Charles Darwin once said of hell:

> I can hardly see how anyone ought to wish Christianity to be true;
> for if so the plain language of the text (Bible) seems to show that the
> men who do not believe, and this would include my father, brother,
> and almost all of my friends, will be everlastingly punished. And
> this is a damnable doctrine.[5]

The notion of hell just seems archaic, offensive, and ridiculous to many people. It is not uncommon to hear, "How can any intelligent person believe in a literal place called hell?" Some find the topic to be an invention of religious people to serve their personal agendas or infatuation with primitive superstition. Perhaps this mentality explains why some pastors would rather not deal with the topic. Others believe that any discussion of such a difficult and sensitive topic should reside with one's parents or immediate family. As I've asked friends, parents, and students if the subject has been addressed in their respective homes, churches, or Christian schools, the vast majority said "no," or that they have only heard a passing reference from time to time.

I remember once hearing an old school, small town Baptist pastor warn his parishioners to "turn or burn" and then describe how people must turn to God for forgiveness or face the punishment of

---

[5] Nora Barlow, ed. *The Autobiography of Charles Darwin, 1809-1882.* (New York: W.W. Norton, 1969), 87.

hell that their sins deserve. That may have been the only time in my life that I heard a sermon about hell, and at the time I wasn't sure if I should cringe, laugh, or cry. I've known some people who have been pushed away from God or a particular church because of that type of preaching. I've known others who have never considered whether or not a literal place called hell might exist. Either way, if hell is a literal place where someone can dwell eternally, should not its reality be considered?

YOLF

Before talking more about hell, let's take a look at the concept of eternity. The idea of eternity seems foolish to those who don't believe in God or any form of life beyond the grave. "Don't bother wasting time daydreaming or fretting about fairytales, fantasies, and things that no one can know for certain," has been the response I've received from some regarding the afterlife. Perhaps the most interesting approach to the topic was demonstrated by a former colleague who used to write the acronymns YOLO and YOLF on his dry erase board at the start of each school year. On the first day of class, new students would come in, sit down, and notice the words written on the board. The teacher would always start class by asking, "How many of you know what the word *YOLO* means?" In unison, the students responded with, "You only live once." He would then say, "How about the word *YOLF*?" Nobody could give the answer.

Actually, YOLF stands for "you only live forever." According to the Bible, each person will live forever, and God has put a longing for eternity in each of our hearts (Ecc. 3:11). It's hardwired. This means that death is not the end but the beginning of eternity. And according to the Bible, the two eternal options are either heaven or hell. If this is true, then some decisions have implications that will last forever.

Some might not agree with the concept of eternity, much less a literal place called hell, but denying the biblical teaching about these subjects does not make them cease to exist. Further, what might the benefits be for those who believe that a graveyard will be their body's final place of rest? Such a conclusion seems pretty pointless and bleak at the end of the day, and even more so at the end of a life.

Saved From What?

The words *saved* and *salvation* can be used and understood in various ways within the contexts of both the Bible and today's culture. I once overheard a banker say, "Jesus saves; so should you." Of course, he was joking. In reference to a boxing or MMA match, you might hear that a fighter was "saved by the bell." Maybe your parent or grandparent "saved" coupons at some point along the way. Distance runners are told to "save" energy for the end of a race.

In relation to Christianity, you've likely heard the question, "Are you saved?" You might be asking, "What does this mean, or what am I being saved from?" Ask five people and you will likely get several different responses. Some believe that "being saved" means to be saved from the devil. Many Christians understand the term to mean being rescued or spared from hell, which in one sense is true, but more clarity is needed. The traditional Christian view has always been that sinners are saved from the wrath of God. The Bible declares that all have sinned and fall short of the glory of God, that no one is righteous, and that the wages of sin leads to spiritual death (Rom. 3:23, 6:23). This means that everyone is guilty of sin whether they realize it or not. It also means that no one is without excuse (Rom. 1:20). It seems pretty straightforward. But why is it that some people really don't seem to care?

The most basic reason why some people seem indifferent or unconcerned about hell is that they are not convinced of being in any form of spiritual danger. It is much easier to dismiss the notion of hell if one does not believe the Bible is truthful and authoritative. As we saw in the chapter about atheism, those who do not believe in God, the Bible, or souls, are certainly not going to believe in hell. This is also the reason why some are bothered by people who believe such a place could exist.

Though the Bible mentions hell, not everyone who believes in the Bible will view hell in the exact same way. In fact, some preachers have either refused to preach about hell, or denied it altogether. They simply cannot fathom God allowing any of his creatures to go to hell. Rob Bell's controversial book *Love Wins* proposes that everyone will end up in heaven (universalism) because of God's love. The assumption is that Christ's death and resurrection will provide everyone entrance to heaven regardless of their lifestyle or views about God. This is an appealing concept, for who wouldn't want to live in the pleasures of sin without any ultimate consequences? Such teaching is not biblical.

Others view hell as a final act of judgment that will eliminate the body and soul of people who do not believe in God. This view of hell is usually referred to as "annihilationism," for upon death, nonbelievers will be annihilated and cease to exist. At first glance, this view can also make sense, especially for people who do not believe in God, souls, or hell. But like universalism, it is not supported by the Bible. There are numerous places in scripture that refer to hell as being eternal (Mark 3:29; 2 Thess. 1:9; Jude 6, 7 & 13; Rev. 14:11).

Obviously, one's conception of hell will determine his or her approach to the topic. The way Christians interpret the biblical references to hell has major implications for the ways in which they might approach their witnessing. Those ignoring the reality of God's eternal wrath aimed at sin are denying what scripture has made clear (we will look at some passages in a moment). Because it seems like a harsh teaching, some Christians do not talk about hell. But those willing only to speak of God's love and grace are choosing to give their listeners only half the gospel. It is important to note that too little or too much emphasis on hell can lead to negative consequences. If someone only hears of judgment and wrath, they may have no desire to hear of God's love and grace; however, failing to warn people of the consequences of sin could prevent them from understanding their need to be rescued.

Rather than adhering to the traditional biblical teaching about hell, some Christians have chosen to interpret the meaning of hell in different ways. Within some of the more progressive circles of Christianity, hell is defined as separation from God. The idea of eternal damnation is not in the equation. Notice what one minister, Oliver Thomas, had to say about the issue:

> Death to the nonbeliever means eternal separation from God, which is hell enough if you ask me. But everlasting torment? The best evidence suggests that this is a human invention designed to scare and manipulate ordinary folk into doing what the church wanted them to do. On the church's worst days, the doctrine of hell was used to extort money. Lots of it. On its best days, hell was used to encourage lives of moral rectitude..... Show people they are loved by God and the members of their congregation and you've won converts for life.[6]

Thomas correctly observes that many people throughout history have used hell as a scare tactic to manipulate others, often causing more harm than good. So, the options for some have been to either avoid discussing hell or redefine its meaning. Both approaches prevent many people from understanding a biblical view of hell. If hell is minimized or neglected to the point of extinction, will people really sense the need to be rescued from anything? If hell does not exist, was Christ's death

---

[6] Rev. Oliver "Buzz" Thomas. *Ten Things Your Minister Wants to Tell You (But Can't Because He Needs the Job)* (New York: St. Martin's Griffin, 2007), 93.

on the cross really necessary? If Christ's sacrificial death did not cul-
minate in victory over death, sin, and hell (which was the reason why
he came and what his resurrection proved), then why should one care?

A reason why some people are indifferent to the gospel is because
sin has been minimized and ignored. More than a half century ago,
C.S. Lewis noticed the widespread neglect of sin, saying, "A recovery
of the old sense of sin is essential to Christianity."[7] Because some sins,
as outlined in scripture, have become a normal, acceptable part of our
culture, when the suggestion that consequences, especially eternal consequences, could somehow be tied to one's sins, most people scoff. R.C.
Sproul rightly points out that, "People do not sense a need for being
rescued because they have never been persuaded of their need for Christ.
People today do not believe that there will be a day of judgment. But
if we believed it, really believed it, the energy of our evangelism would
increase a hundredfold."[8]

Not only has the gospel been watered down in recent years, but
so has the urgency to share it. Despite the biblical mandate for all
Christians to share the Good News, it has become increasingly less
common (Matt. 28:18-20). Think about it for a moment. How many
times in your life has someone shared the gospel with you? Did that
gospel presentation contain anything about sin or hell? I can count the
number of times on one hand. If you are a Christian, how many times
have you shared the "full" gospel with someone else?

The Bible declares that, "Jesus came to warn and rescue sinners,"
which explains why he spoke of a literal hell so often (1 Tim. 1:15).
If people don't sense the presence of danger, especially eternal danger,
they will likely not sense their need for a Savior to rescue them from it.
This is why believers are to share the full gospel, which contains both

[7] C.S. Lewis, *The Problem of Pain.* (San Francisco: Harper, 2001), 50.
[8] R.C. Sproul, *Saved From What?* (Wheaton, IL: Crossway Books, 2002), 23.

the bad and Good News. It's not something you jump right into, but hopefully it comes up once you've earned the right to be heard. It has been said that someone will not listen to what you say until they know how much you care. With such a complicated topic like hell, this saying has never been more applicable.

Because the Bible declares that hell is a real, eternal, potential destination for every person, Christians need to think about ways to help people realize that there will be consequences for sin. The Apostle Paul warned Christians in the earliest days of the church about the danger of the judgment day:

> Because of your stubbornness and your unrepentant heart, you are storing up wrath against yourself for the day of God's wrath when his righteous judgment will be revealed. God will give to each person according to what he has done. To those who by persistence in doing good seek glory, honor and immortality, he will give eternal life. But for those who are self-seeking and who reject the truth and follow evil, there will be wrath and anger. (Romans 2:5-8)

The idea that "God will give to each person according to what he or she has done" is not a popular notion in the world today, but it is what the Bible teaches. Not only does the Bible teach it, but it also spells out the fact that no one can believe the Good News if Christians don't share it:

> How, then, can they call on the one they have not believed in? And how can they believe in the one of whom they have not heard? And how can they hear without someone preaching to them? And how can they preach unless they are sent? As it is written, 'How beautiful are the feet of those who bring the good news'. (Romans 10:13-15)

The End is the Beginning

When German theologian Dietrich Bonhoeffer was being led to his execution at a concentration camp because of his opposition to Hitler's regime, his fellow prisoners heard him exult, "For me this is not the end, but the beginning of life."[9] What if death is not the end, but the gateway to an afterlife? At funerals, it is common to hear people reference the deceased person with phrases like, "She's in a better place" or "He has gone home." What is meant by *home* or *a better place?*

Christians believe that after a person physically dies, his or her soul and resurrected body will end up spending eternity either in heaven or hell. Eventually, God will create a new heaven and a new earth for Christians to enjoy (Rev. 21). The Bible and tradition have taught this for centuries.[10] Most people want some version of heaven to exist, and Christians point to a number of passages that refer to such a place. Before his death, Jesus said to his disciples, "In my father's house are many rooms; if it were not so, I would have told you. I am going there to prepare a place for you" (John 14:2). The Apostle Paul said that, "to be absent from the body is to be present with the Lord" (2 Cor. 5:8).

For many Christians, believing in hell has helped them to make sense of evil and all that is wrong with the world. Embracing this truth

---

[9] Dietrich Bonhoeffer. *Life Together: The Classic Exploration of Faith in Community*, trans. John W. Doberstein (New York: HarperCollins, 1954), 13.

[10] The Roman Catholic Church believes in a place called "Purgatory" and defines it in the *Catechism of the Catholic Church* as a place where God's elect "after death can undergo purification, so as to achieve the holiness necessary to enter the joy of heaven" (1997 edition, par. 1030-31). The Catholic Church has cited the Apocryphal book 2 Maccabees 12:39-45, as well as 1 Corinthians 3:11-15, to support the doctrine of Purgatory. Many Catholics believe that the souls of those detained in Purgatory can receive aid and a reduction in their time there as Christians offer prayers on their behalf. Theologian Peter Kreeft refers to purgatory as "God's loving parental discipline, heaven's porch, heaven's incubator, and heaven's washroom." See Peter Kreeft. *Catholic Christianity: A Complete Catechism of Catholic Beliefs Based on the Catechism of the Catholic Church.* (San Francisco: Ignatius Press, 2001), 149-150. The vast majority of Protestant Christians do not believe in Purgatory, claiming that it is based on the tradition of the Roman Catholic Church, not the Bible.

has enabled many Christians to use the frustrations, disappointments, injustices, and challenges of life to increase their desire for the time when everything will be made right. I remember a pastor once saying, "If hell does not exist, I want my money back, for it does not seem loving or fair for God to allow the most heinous crimes to remain unpunished forever. There has to be retribution for all the evil in the world or nothing makes sense." According to the Bible, in the end there are only two eternal options. Regardless of how you might view the concept of spending an eternity in either heaven or hell at the moment, it seems that a closer look would be worth your time now.

Thoughts About Hell

When you think about hell, what comes to mind? Perhaps a scene from a movie or cartoon? Most people don't want to think about it—like the concept of sin, the idea of a real hell is not very popular. It just seems better to avoid the subject rather than offend someone. This has not always been the case. Prior to the past half century, the subject of hell occupied a much more prominent place in art, literature, and pulpits across the world. Most people lived as if hell actually existed. The orthodox, traditional view concerning what the Bible teaches about hell is that someone cannot clearly understand the Good News of Jesus Christ without first understanding the bad news that results from being separated from God because of sin.

Influential New York City pastor Tim Keller once said, "Unless I think about hell, I'm losing sight of God's love."[11] Most people do not see the terms *love* and *hell* as having anything to do with each other, but when we understand what hell is and why it exists,

---

[11] https://www.youtube.com "Isn't the God of Christianity an Angry Judge?"

Keller's statement starts to make more sense. One's conception of hell is absolutely essential to understanding God's love. The true source of God's love was demonstrated most clearly through Christ's death and resurrection. It was the ultimate act of love in the drama of all dramas, and when people understand the true nature of sin and hell having eternal consequences, the love demonstrated by Christ's incarnation, crucifixion and resurrection becomes even more astonishing. The Bible declares that if Christ has not been raised from the dead then faith is worthless and people remain in their sins (1 Cor. 15). The sad reality is that most people don't sense any reason to believe in Jesus Christ and why he came, much less try to live as he did, ask for forgiveness or believe that there is any reason to repent of wrongdoing. When people are told God loves them so much that they can freely do as they please and spend eternity in heaven regardless of their actions, the cost of Christ's death is minimized. Such thinking also contradicts the numerous passages in scripture that condemn sin and plead for repentance.

The Bible makes clear that God loves sinners and despises sin, but some people have trouble understanding how God can be loving, yet also be described as being angry and filled with wrath. Keller provides an excellent explanation:

> All loving persons are sometimes filled with wrath, not just de- spite of, but because of their love. If you love a person and you see someone ruining them—even they themselves--you get angry.... The Bible says that God's wrath flows from his love and delight in creation. He is angry at evil and injustice because it is destroying peace and integrity.[12]

Clearly, anger can result from love, and because God is loving, he

---

[12] Tim Keller. *The Reason for God: Belief in an Age of Skepticism.* (New York: Riverhead Books, 2008), 75-76.

is angry at the evil, sin, and injustice that permeate the world. Because of God's love, he did do something about it. It is described in what some consider to be the most famous passage in the Bible:

> For God so loved the world that he gave his only begotten son, that whoever believes in him should not perish but have eternal life. For God did not send his Son into the world to condemn the world, but in order that the world might be saved through him. Whoever believes in him is not condemned, but whoever does not believe is condemned already, because he has not believed in the name of the only Son of God (John 3:16-17).

Apart from what is revealed in the Bible, I doubt that anyone has provided a better glimpse of hell than the famous eighteenth-century preacher Jonathan Edwards, best known for his sermon called *Sinners in the Hands of an Angry God*. But sermons that addressed hell were not unique to Jonathan Edwards or his times. In fact, Edwards learned from both his father and grandfather the power of hellfire preaching. Edwards's famous maternal grandfather, Reverend Solomon Stoddard, once stated, "When men don't preach much about the danger of damnation, there is want of good preaching."[13] Stoddard, Edwards, and many other ministers of the Puritan tradition preached "hellfire" sermons during times of religious lethargy because they believed God used it to bring about spiritual awakenings. Preaching about hell was an essential part of their evangelism. Edwards explained:

> I am not afraid to tell sinners who are most sensible of their misery, that their case is indeed as miserable as they think it to be, and a thousand times more so; for this is the truth…Ministers ought to act as co-workers with God…and strike while the iron is hot…All

---

[13] Cited in Wilson H. Kimnach, "The Sermons: Concepts and Execution," in *The Princeton Companion to Jonathan Edwards.* Ed. Sang Hyun Lee. (Princeton, NJ: Princeton University Press, 2005), 252.

are by nature the children of wrath, and heirs of hell—and every one that has not been born again, whether he be young or old, is exposed every moment to eternal destruction...Why should we conceal the truth from them?[14]

Though hellfire sermons were often the primary catalysts to instigate spiritual revivals, it is important to note that these types of sermons were not designed merely to scare people out of a future hell, but also to promote piety in the present so that God's glory would be displayed as his people responded in faith to the circumstances of life.[15] One of the best examples of Jonathan Edwards's numerous hellfire sermons is called *The Torments of Hell are Exceedingly Great.* Some have argued that the gruesome imagery displayed in that homily was more alarming than the imagery found in *Sinners in the Hands of an Angry God.*[16] The outlook for unrepentant people outside of Christ described in the sermon was rather bleak:

> You shall have no hope of ever being delivered; when after you shall have worn out a thousand more such ages, yet you shall have no hope, but shall know that you are not one whit nearer to the end of your torments; but that still there are the same groans, the same shrieks, the same doleful cries, incessantly to be made by you, and that the smoke of your torment shall still ascend up, forever and ever.[17]

Wow, that's intense! You may be thinking that Edwards used such

---

[14] Jonathan Edwards, "Some Thoughts on the Present Revival of Religion," in *The Works of Jonathan Edwards,* Vol. 1, 392-393.

[15] Frank Lambert. *Inventing the Great Awakening.* (Princeton, NJ: Princeton University Press, 1999), 64-65.

[16] Wilson H. Kimnach believes that Sinners is more of an awakening sermon with a "proto-eschatological concern consumed with the here and now," more so than a true hellfire sermon. See "The Sermons: Concept and Execution," in *The Princeton Companion to Jonathan Edwards,* p. 253. Also see Glenn R. Kreider, "Sinners in the Hands of a Gracious God."

[17] Edmund C. Stedman, ed. *A Library of American Literature: From the Earliest Settlement to the Present Time, Vol. II.* (New York: Charles L. Webster & Co., 1891), 394.

graphic imagery to scare his listeners into making an emotional decision. My first exposure to this hellfire sermon sparked many questions: Does hell really exist, and if so, can it really be that bad? Does the Bible speak of hell in such an exaggerated, graphic way? How often did Edwards and other ministers during that time preach about hell? How did people react to such preaching?

Sinners in the Hands of An Angry God

Sinners in the Hands of an Angry God has appeared in most American literature anthologies over the past fifty years. For many students, this sermon is their only exposure to Jonathan Edwards and the concept of hell. Unfortunately, many textbooks and teachers caricature Edwards as a sadistic, doom-and-gloom preacher of the Puritan tradition who literally tried to scare the hell out of sinners so that they might end up in heaven. But Edwards has been lauded as the greatest theologian and philosopher that America has ever produced, and *Sinners in the Hands of an Angry God* has been one of the sermons most responsible for generating thoughts of hell over the centuries.

What many people do not know is that Edwards not only aimed to awaken concern by using rhetorical precision to describe the horrors of hell in this sermon, but that he ultimately wanted to help people realize their dire spiritual predicament. His aim was to stir the heart, to stimulate the soul, and to turn the whole person to a devoted search for the springs of God's grace.[18] Like his predecessors, Edwards believed that theological explanations regarding such terrors were necessary in order to prepare listeners to embrace the gospel.[19] Notice how Edwards's

[18] Edwin H. Cady. "The Artistry of Jonathan Edwards." *New England Quarterly*. Vol. 22, No. 1 (March 1949), 62.

[19] Richard Lischer. ed. *The Company of Preachers: Wisdom on Preaching Augustine to the Present*. (Grand Rapids, MI: Eerdmans, 2002), 120.

sermon is filled with graphic imagery describing God's wrath toward sinners:

> The God that holds you over the pit of hell, much as one holds a spider, or some loathsome insect, over the fire, abhors you, and is dreadfully provoked; his wrath towards you burns like fire; he looks upon you as worthy of nothing else but to be cast into the fire...you have offended him infinitely more than ever a stubborn rebel did his prince: and yet 'tis nothing but his hand that holds you from falling into the fire every moment: 'tis to be ascribed to nothing else that you did not go to hell last night...but that God's hand has held you up: there is no other reason to be given why you have not gone to hell since you have sat here in the house of God, provoking his pure eyes by your sinful wicked manner of attending his solemn worship: yea, there is nothing else that is to be given as a reason why you don't this very moment drop into hell. Oh sinner! Consider the fearful danger you are in.

> How dreadful is the state of those that are daily and hourly in the danger of this great wrath and infinite misery! But this is the dismal case of every soul in this congregation that has not been born again, however moral or strict, sober and religious, they may otherwise be. Oh, that you would consider it, whether you be young or old![20]

Based solely on these frightening passages, it is no wonder that people have been awakened by Edwards's vivid imagery. However, we must keep in mind that the emphasis and central theme of this sermon, and Edwards's entire ministry, was the grace of God. The accent in his sermons was not on the flames (at least not permanently) but on God's hand of mercy that is holding unrepentant sinners from falling into that place of eternal torment and devastation.

If people focus solely on punishment, they will fail to recognize the pardon so clearly provided for sinners to escape their horrible

---

[20] Jonathan Edwards, *Sinners in the Hands of an Angry God and Other Writings.* (Nashville, TN: Thomas Nelson, 2000), 11-15.

predicament—the amazing grace of God offered freely to all who repent and place their faith in Christ. The Bible declares that every person is born with a sinful nature and is therefore an object of God's wrath because of the punishment that their sinful crimes deserve (Rom. 1:18-24, Eph. 2:8-10). Edwards held that the root of human sinfulness was antagonism towards God, but he also understood that God's gracious provision has always been to preserve life.[21] Notice what the Apostle Paul had to say about this matter:

> At just the right time, when we were still powerless, Christ died for the ungodly.... God demonstrates his own love for us in this: While we were still sinners, Christ died for us.... For if we were God's enemies, we were reconciled to him through the death of his Son, how much more, having been reconciled, shall we be saved through his life. (Romans 5:6-10)

Edwards believed that God's infinite love, mercy, and grace would be magnified once sinners had a clear understanding of God's mounting wrath that would soon be unleashed as a consequence of their sin. Yale scholar Harry Stout points out how, "Edwards believed, for a moment anyway, that one could get to eternal life only after first being scared to death." He goes on to say that, "During the Great Awakening in the 1740s, hell, in all its fury and torture, would have to be enlisted if heaven was ever to be gained."[22] So for Edwards and other preachers in the Puritan tradition, the bad news of God's wrath is what enabled people to understand the good news of God's grace.

Since the late eighteenth century, the emphasis on hell in preaching, and in everyday discourse, has continued to wane. Both sin and hell have been minimized and trivialized more so with each passing

---

[21] Mark A. Noll. *America's God: From Jonathan Edwards to Abraham Lincoln.* (New York: Oxford University Press, 2002), 24. Glenn R. Kreider. *Sinners in the Hands of a Gracious God.* www.bible.org.

[22] Harry S. Stout, "Edwards and Revival," in *Understanding Jonathan Edwards: An Introduction to America's Theologian.* Ed. Gerald R. McDermott. (New York: Oxford, 2009). 48.

generation. However, there will always be preachers like Edwards who realize the bad news enables sinners to understand their need to embrace the Good News. Notice how Edwards followed the climax of his sermon by concluding with an emphasis on the love, mercy, and grace of God. After pronouncing the guilty verdict, Edwards knew his audience would be ready to hear about the extraordinary possibility of receiving a gracious pardon:

> And now you have an extraordinary opportunity, a day wherein Christ has thrown the door of mercy wide open, and stands in calling and crying with a loud voice to poor sinners; a day wherein many are flocking to him, and pressing into the kingdom of God. Many are daily coming from the east, west, north and south; many that were very lately in the same miserable condition that you are in, are now in a happy state, with their hearts filled with love to him who has loved them, and washed them from their sins in his own blood, and rejoicing in hope of the glory of God. How awful is it to be left behind at such a day! To see so many others feasting, while you are perishing! To see so many rejoicing and singing for joy of heart, while you have cause to mourn for sorrow of heart. How can you rest one moment in such a condition?"[23]

Edwards's preaching of hellfire sermons invoked both fear and hope, like the proverbial surgeon who must inflict pain before his patient can be healed. Many people fail to take into account the element of hope found at the conclusion of sermons like *Sinners in the Hands of An Angry God*. Edwards constantly reminded his listeners that they truly lived on the edge of eternity, and that it was utter folly to become too preoccupied with mere worldly concerns.[24] If he frequently tried to shake his audiences' spiritual complacency by preaching the terrors of hell, he invariably coupled it with the assurance that "there is a Savior provided, who is excellent and glorious; who has shed his

---

[23] *Sinners in the Hands of an Angry God,* 16.

precious blood for sinners, and is in every way sufficient to save them; who stands ready to receive them."[25]

Contrary to popular opinion, Edwards spent much less time depicting the wrath of God than he did preparing sermons about God's love, mercy, and grace. He never doubted that hell exists to which sinners go after death, but that consideration was a footnote.[26] Though he regularly preached about the reality of hell, the majority of his sermons dealt with the greatness and glory of God, the utter dependence of sinful humanity on God for salvation, and the beauty of the life of holiness.[27] Edwards knew much about hell, but knew heaven better. John Gerstner explains Edwards's view of heaven and hell in this way:

> If he spoke more of hell, it was only because he feared more people were going there, and he desired to set them on their way to heaven. Even as he defended the justice of God in the damnation of sinners, he triumphantly extolled the Divine and everlasting mercy in the salvation of saints.[28]

Perhaps the most important aspect of Edwards's delivery style was how he often succeeded in causing his listeners to think about the punishment their sins warranted, which in turn helped them to realize their need to be rescued from God's wrath by God's grace.

This type of preaching is rare in most churches today. Obviously, a sermon of this nature would not be well received in most contexts. I am not suggesting that it could or should, for unlike the time in

[25] Francis J. Bremer. *The Puritan Experiment: New England Society from Bradford to Edwards*. (Lebanon, NH: University Press of New England, 1995), 232.

[26] Perry Miller. *Jonathan Edwards*. (New York: William Sloan, 1949), 149. Edwin H. Cady pointed out that fire-imagery displayed in *Sinners* amounts to little more than a quarter of the total (about 25) figures, in "The Artistry of Jonathan Edwards," *New England Quarterly* 22 (March 1949).

[27] Mark A. Noll. *A History of Christianity in the United States and Canada*. (Grand Rapids: Eerdmans, 1992), 97. Also see George Marsden. *Jonathan Edwards: A Life*. (New Haven: Yale University Press, 2003), 165.

[28] John H. Gerstner, *Jonathan Edwards on Heaven and Hell* (Morgan, PA: Soli Deo Gloria, 1998), 9.

which Edwards lived, most people do not have the biblical framework necessary to understand such preaching. However, if one believes in the Bible and the very words of Christ, understanding the reality of hell and the final judgment should be a top priority.

Hell in the New Testament

Since we are talking about something that lasts forever, one should want to get it right. Though no one can possibly understand precisely what hell might be like, the Bible has always provided the clearest description. The topic of hell was very important to Jesus, and he often warned people about it. In fact, Jesus spoke of hell more than most other topics. His very first sermon focused on warning people about hell, and he spoke more about hell than everyone else in the Bible combined (Matt. chapters 5, 10, 18, 23). Because Christians are Christ's ambassadors, what does it say about believers who refuse to discuss the reality of hell? Because Christians claim that the Bible contains the very words of Almighty God, how should they interpret the many references to judgment and hell that are contained within the Bible, especially the New Testament?

As we discussed in the Bible chapter, scripture often uses symbolic language to describe that which is beyond what our finite minds can comprehend. In relation to hell, what is described in the Bible is likely far worse than any of us can imagine. One image used for picturing hell was a familiar, dreadful place called *Gehenna*, which was a literal trash dump located south of Jerusalem. Everyone was familiar with the horrific pagan history of the place, as well as the stench from the smoke of constant burning piles of trash in Gehenna (Mark 9:47-48; Matt. 5:22-30; 9:43-47; 10:28; 18:9).[29] In context, Jesus was warning his listeners to strive for

---

[29] Because the site of Gehenna was once a place where pagans sacrificed children, it eventually became a garbage heap because nothing else could occupy a place with such a dreadful past.

peace, or else all of Jerusalem would become like its garbage dump. But, many have also pointed to Gehenna as a symbolic description of what hell may be like. The Bible also uses the phrase "lake of fire" to describe the place of eternal punishment for the wicked (Revelation 20:12-15). Regardless of whether one interprets "lake of fire" literally or metaphorically, it does not sound pleasant by any stretch of the imagination.

We cannot know the full extent of what hell will be like, but we can be certain that it is not a situation or place in which one would want to experience forever. There are various opinions about hell in society, but many are not based on what has been revealed in scripture. Learning the biblical perspective about hell is absolutely essential to realize the consequences of sin, need for grace, and the ability to live with the peace of forgiveness and promise of hope. The Bible states that one's eternal destination is determined by whether or not he or she embraces Jesus Christ as Lord and Savior. This is not a popular doctrine in many segments of the world, but it is what the Bible teaches. Both the final judgment and hell are repeatedly emphasized throughout the New Testament.[30] Below are some of the explicit references:

Matthew 5:29-30

If your right eye causes you to sin, gouge it out and throw it away. It is better for you to lose one part of your body than for your whole body to be thrown into hell. And if your right hand causes you to sin, cut if off and throw it away. It is better for you to lose one part of your body than for your whole body to go into hell.

---

[30] See N.T. Wright. *Following Jesus: Biblical Reflections on Discipleship*. (Grand Rapids: Eerdmans, 1994) 95-103. Wright mentions that a few warnings in the New Testament referring to God's actions within the world and history (Mark 13) have been incorrectly interpreted by Christians to describe hell. Scholars who do not believe in the authority and divinely inspired nature of the Bible argue that none of the passages in the Bible refer to a literal hell. The assumption is that biblical authors borrowed stories from other ancient sources (such as *The Epic of Gilgamesh*), and that generations of Christians have been guilty of promoting the myth of hell.

Matthew 25:45-46

He (Jesus) will reply, "I tell you the truth, whatever you did not do for one of the least of these, you did not do for me. Then they will go away to eternal punishment, but the righteous to eternal life."

Romans 2:5-8

But because of your stubbornness and your unrepentant heart, you are storing up wrath against yourself for the day of God's wrath, when his righteous judgment will be revealed. God will give to each person according to what he has done. To those who by persistence in doing good seek glory, honor and immortality, he will give eternal life. But for those who are self-seeking and who reject the truth and follow evil, there will be wrath and anger.

2 Thessalonians 1:7-10

This will happen when the Lord Jesus is revealed from heaven in blazing fire with his powerful angels. He will punish those who do not know God and do not obey the gospel of our Lord Jesus. They will be punished with everlasting destruction and shut out from the presence of the Lord and from the glory of his might on the day he comes to be glorified in his holy people and to be marveled at among all those who have believed.

There are many other passages claiming that God will judge both the righteous and the wicked (Ecc. 3:15-17, 13:36-43; Matt. 10:28; John 5:28-29; Rom. 1:18-20; Heb. 10:26-27; 2 Thess. 1:6-10; 2 Pet. 2:2). Theologian R.C. Sproul sums up well the importance of what scripture conveys:

> If people understood two things—that God is holy, and that sin is an offense against his holiness—then they would be breaking down the doors of churches, pleading, "What must I do to be saved?" We may like to think that we don't need a Savior, but the atonement and the cross of Christianity operate on the primary assumption that we are in desperate need of salvation. That assumption may

not be shared by our modern culture, but that does not lessen the reality of the need.[31]

If one believes the Bible, then there is really no way around the issue. Though no one knows exactly what hell will be like, many have come to respect the imagery provided by C.S. Lewis:

> I wouldn't put the question in the form, "do I believe in an actual Hell." One's own mind is actual enough. If it doesn't seem fully actual now that is because you can always escape from it a bit into the physical world—look out of the window, smoke a cigarette, go to sleep. But when there is nothing for you but your own mind (no body to go to sleep, no books or landscape, nor sounds, no drugs) it will be as actual as—as—well, as *a coffin is actual to a man buried alive.*[32]

Another Oxford professor, John Lennox, claimed that in hell people "will remain in a fixed, spiritually morbid state, without relief or hope for eternity."[33] Imagine an eternity without love, friendship, mercy, consolation, or reconciliation. Imagine an eternity filled only with loneliness and despair. If the Bible and the church's teaching about hell is true, then everyone should take this doctrine very seriously.

And Justice for All

So we've established that God is loving and that his displeasure with sin led to Christ's death as payment for the punishment that humanity's sin deserved, but what are we to make of the lack of justice in the world? Some have proposed that hell could somehow provide retribution for injustice. Simply wake up in the morning, tune in to the

[31] Sproul. *Saved From What?*, 46-47.

[32] C.S. Lewis. *The Letters of C.S. Lewis to Arthur Greeves* (13 May 1946).

[33] David Gooding and John Lennox. *Key Bible Concepts.* (Coleraine, Ireland: Myrtlefield House), 134.

news and go about your day, and you will notice that things are not as they should be. It is a broken world, full of pain and suffering. When we or people we know are mistreated, we want justice. When evil and sin run rampant without any apparent ramifications or consequences, our hearts cry for justice. Unfortunately, despite the best efforts of law enforcement and court systems, we all know that justice is not rendered in many situations. This is saddening, maddening, and wrong. There are people in the world right now who are experiencing pain that most of us cannot fathom.

In no way can or should the pain, suffering, misery, and frustration associated with injustice be minimized or forgotten, but when one realizes that ultimate justice was accomplished on the cross (and will be fully realized in eternity) a semblance of peace and comfort can be attained now, even amid the scars and pain. It is the reason why so many Christians, including countless believers who were martyred for their faith, could face mistreatment, imprisonment, and even death, with confidence. The Apostle Peter encouraged Christians who were being severely persecuted:

> Dear friends, do not be surprised at the painful trial you are suffering, as though something strange were happening to you. But rejoice that you participate in the sufferings of Christ, so that you may be overjoyed when his glory is revealed. If you are insulted because of the name of Christ, you are blessed, for the Spirit of glory and of God rests on you...If you suffer as a Christian, do not be ashamed, but praise God that you bear that name. For it is time for judgment to begin with the family of God; and if it begins with us, what will the outcome be for those who do not obey the gospel of God? (1 Peter 4:12-17)

Many of the biblical writers implored those facing injustice to trust in the Lord's promises, not only God's promise of everlasting life, but also his promise that one day every crime and form of injustice would be vindicated. The Bible makes it clear that there will be an unavoidable judgment or "second death" that everyone will face, and that God will hold every person accountable for every sin ever committed (Ps. 145:17-20). This should bring great hope to all who believe. Those suffering persecution or injustice, even people who do not believe in God, want this to be true. This is the reason why the historical reality of Christ's birth, life, death, and resurrection from the dead is such good news. It is the reason billions of people celebrate the incarnation at Christmas each year—for God humbled himself and took on flesh to dwell among his sinful creatures (Phil. 2:8). Jesus not only dwelled among humanity, but he faced injustice, suffered, and died for the sin of every person who has ever lived, including you and me. This was not plan B, but God's perfect plan all along. It was a tragic, yet beautiful example of true love. Without Jesus dying to atone for our sins, ultimate justice could not occur, and the guilt and punishment for our sin would last forever. That would be hell.

There is a lot of truth in the rock band AC/DC's song "Highway to Hell," for without the gospel we would all be on that road. It is worth repeating—the Good News guarantees justice and hope for all who believe that Jesus, who was perfectly innocent of any sin, became sin for us, and bore the wrath that our sins deserve (2 Cor. 5:21; Gal. 3:13). Christ's death and resurrection atoned for the sins of everyone who believes. It is freely offered to us because it cost Christ everything.

If you do not benefit in any way from the rest of this book, I urge you to investigate the life, death, and resurrection of Jesus. No credible historian of antiquity denies that a historical figure named Jesus of Nazareth lived, had a following, and was killed by crucifixion. You owe it to yourself to consider who Jesus was, how he lived, why he died, and what his resurrection means for you. Though it will cost you everything, there is no greater joy than knowing Christ, striving to become more like him, and helping others to do the same.

Salvation came at the enormous price of Christ's death, but it is freely given to those who embrace it by grace through faith (Eph. 2:8-10). It is all about God's grace (unmerited favor). If grace could be inherited, purchased, or earned, it would no longer be grace. It may seem too good to be true, but it is true. The bad news about hell actually made the Good News necessary, and it helps us to understand why Jesus so often warned people about hell. If such a place does not exist, then why would Jesus have talked about it so much?

Each person must decide to either reject or accept the most extraordinary gift ever made available. Those who choose to reject Christ are also rejecting his gracious pardon. People are certainly free to reject Jesus now, but in the end every knee will bow and tongue confess that Jesus Christ is Lord. Those who receive God's free gift of grace will experience joy now, and spend eternity rejoicing in the wonder and beauty of his presence. This is what the Bible teaches, and it helps us to see how belief in the reality of hell can actually bring peace, comfort, and hope. Take note of an observation by C.S. Lewis:

> There are two kinds of people in the end: those who say to God, "Thy will be done," and those to whom God says, in the end, "Thy will be done." All that are in Hell, choose it. Without that self-choice, there could be no Hell. No soul that seriously and constantly desires joy will ever miss it. Those who seek, find. To those who knock, it is opened.[34]

It is important to understand that God does not send anyone to hell, but it is the destination of those who choose to go there. In *The Problem of Pain*, Lewis states, "I willingly believe that the damned are, in one sense, successful, rebels to the end; that the doors of hell are

[34] C.S. Lewis. *The Great Divorce.* (New York: Touchstone, 1974), 73-75.

locked on the inside."[35] The *Catechism of the Catholic Church* declares, "Man is made to live in communion with God," therefore, hell is the "state of definitive self-exclusion from communion with God."[36] People who have rejected God are essentially already experiencing hell because their sin has separated them from God, but eventually the ability to know and experience God's love and forgiveness will no longer be possible. They've already chosen to shut God out of their lives, and at some point the separation will become permanent. This is why Tim Keller essentially defines hell as "the trajectory of a soul, living a self-absorbed, self-centered life, going on forever and ever."[37] Keller is saying, just like C.S. Lewis, that people have a choice to make all along. Those who choose to reject God are choosing to remain on the highway to hell.

At some point every person will be called into the courtroom of God, for the Bible declares that everyone "is destined to die once, and after that face judgment" (Heb. 9:27). The final judgment will be thorough, and the punishment will fit the crime. Everyone will stand before the perfect, righteous Judge, and give an account for everything that has been said and done, for it is written: "As surely as I live, says the Lord, every knee will bow before me; every tongue will confess to God" (Rom. 14:11). At that moment, every person will recognize Christ's authority as ruler of all, but not everyone will have believed it. Based on the Bible's teaching, hell will be the worst news imaginable for those who have not understood and embraced the gospel. No matter what we've done, seemingly big or small, the final verdict declares every person guilty and separated from God. That is bad news! We need to give it serious attention!

---

[35] C.S. Lewis. *The Problem of Pain.* (New York: Mcmillan, 1962), 127.

[36] *Catechism of the Catholic Church.* (New York: Doubleday, 1995), 45 & 1033.

[37] Keller, *The Reason for God,* 79.

The Good News is that the righteous Judge is waiting now to forgive all who are willing to receive his gracious pardon. Regardless of how bad you think you are, how distant God may seem to be, or if you feel unworthy of God's forgiveness, God really does love and cherish you, for after all, he created you! He also died for you. He loves you the way you are, just as you are, but wants you to repent of your sins, receive forgiveness, grow in faith, and experience the joy of following him. Salvation cannot be earned. It must be received by faith alone. The Bible declares, "For it is by grace you have been saved, through faith. And this is not from yourselves, it is the gift of God" (Eph. 2:8-9). In another place, scripture reveals that, "Without faith it is impossible to please God" (Heb. 11:6). With faith, however, all things are possible (Matt. 19:23). Believers experience abundant life, and it starts at the moment complete trust is placed in Christ. By faith, it is available at this moment.

Hell is an offensive topic to most people, but it is what the Bible teaches. It should be discussed, but very prayerfully and carefully. Religion without grace leads only to legalism and despair. Life without grace can lead to hell. The subject of hell should never be used as a scare tactic to manipulate someone into making a decision because they fear God or hell. One's relationship with God and eternal destination are between God and that person. Though the reality of hell is rather frightening, Christ wants everyone to experience peace and forgiveness. If people properly understand God's justice, they should wholeheartedly embrace his love and grace. Salvation is not about accepting Christ as a spiritual insurance policy to escape eternal damnation. Being a Christian should be about knowing and loving Jesus, and living in his mercy and grace, not trying to avoid hell.

Questions for Discussion:

1. Do you believe that each person's soul will live forever? Why or why not?

2. Why do you think some people are reluctant to believe in a literal hell?

3. When you think about the term *hell*, what comes to mind?

4. Why do you think many Christians, including ministers and teachers, seldom discuss the topic of hell?

5. Why do you think Jesus mentioned hell so often in the New Testament?

6. If hell is one of two eternal destinations for every person who has ever lived, including you and me, how should this affect one's desire to talk about hell and also share the Good News?

7. Do you have any questions, doubts, or reservations about hell?

8. If hell is a literal, eternal destination, how might this change your thinking and approach to life?

For Further Reading:

Alan W. Gomes. *40 Questions About Heaven and Hell.* Grand Rapids: Kregel Academic, 2018.

Francis Chan and Preston Sprinkle. *Erasing Hell.* Colorado Springs: David C. Cook, 2011.

Timothy Keller. *The Reason for God: Belief in an Age of Skepticism.* New York: Riverhead Books, 2008.

TALKING TO GOD

There is a big difference between adhering to a religion and having a relationship with God. Religion often leads to legalism, whereas a relationship creates love and trust. Christianity is not about religion. It's about a personal relationship between creatures and the Creator of the universe. As we've seen throughout this book, this relationship is made possible when we embrace Christ as Lord and Savior. Our personal relationship with the living God starts with a prayer, and prayer allows that relationship to grow and continue forever. Imagine what it would be like to have the ear of Almighty God. When we choose to pray, we are exercising this extraordinary privilege. The goal of prayer, therefore, should be to communicate and fellowship with God.

A recent national survey revealed that 55 percent of adults pray on a daily basis, with 20 percent of that group claiming no formal religious affiliation.[1] Although most people find value in prayer, many people choose not to pray. Some don't think it could be beneficial,

---

[1] https://www.pewforum.org/religious-landscape-study/frequency-of-prayer

while others don't know how or what to pray. If you're uncertain about the nature of and need for prayer, you are certainly not alone. The earliest and closest followers of Jesus needed advice about how to pray as well. The main goal of this chapter is to provide a basic overview of prayer and encourage you to pray.

Allow me the privilege of sharing what some Christian leaders from previous generations had to say about prayer. Second-century church father Tertullian viewed prayer as "the wall of faith that provides protection from the evil one."[2] Sixteenth-century Swiss reformer John Calvin defined prayer as "the chief exercise of faith by which believers daily receive God's benefits."[3]

Puritan pastor John Owen defined prayer as "the whole of the Christian life, involving both the objective (what we believe) and the subjective (the act of believing)—it is a gift, a spiritual faculty of exercising faith, love, reverence, fear, delight, and other graces, in a way of vocal requests, supplications and praises unto God."[4] Richard Baxter, another famous Puritan, exclaimed, "The real change that is made by prayer is on ourselves!"[5] Charles Spurgeon, the "Prince of Preachers," described prayer as "the soul talking to God."[6] Theologian Karl Barth viewed prayer as "going toward God, asking him to give us what we lack—strength, courage, serenity, prudence—asking him to teach us how to obey the law and accomplish the commandments."[7] Famous evangelist Billy Graham once said:

[2] Quoted in Donald W. Bercot, ed., *A Dictionary of Early Christian Beliefs*. (Peabody, MA: Hendrickson, 1998), 530.

[3] John Calvin, *Institutes of the Christian Religion*, ed. by John T. McNeill. (Louisville, KY: Westminster John Knox Press, 2006), (3.20.1).

[4] Sinclair B. Ferguson. *John Owen on the Christian Life*. (Carlisle, PA: Banner of Truth, 2001), 225.

[5] Ibid., 217.

[6] Charles Spurgeon. *The Power in Prayer*. (New Kensington, PA: Whitaker House, 1996), 170.

[7] Karl Barth. *Prayer*. (Louisville: Westminster Knox Press, 2002), 11.

Prayer, at its deepest level, is fellowship with God: enjoying His company, waiting upon His will, thanking Him for His mercies, committing our lives to Him, talking to Him about other people as well as ourselves, and listening in the silence for what He has to say to us. Prayer is more than a wish; it is the voice of faith directed to God.[8]

John Wesley, founder of the Methodist Church, said, "God does nothing but in answer to prayer. Every new victory which a soul gains is the effect of a new prayer. The greatest hindrance of holiness is a lack of persistent prayer."[9] Prayer is an act of obedience designed for God's glory and our good.

It is important to understand who and what are involved when praying. Have you thought much about what you approach when you pray? The throne of grace. Have you thought about who sits on that throne? None other than Almighty God, the one who created and sustains the universe, the author and perfecter of faith (Hebrews 12:2). Famous Scottish minister James Steward explains:

> Prayer is a tremendous act—approaching the presence of an infinitely holy God—that it is simply not good enough to have no method about it—with a kind of hit-or-miss casualness. Think of who it is we are coming to.[10]

Prayer places us in the presence of our Creator, the one who knows us best and loves us most despite anything we've said or done. Prayer changes things, especially the one who chooses to pray. No matter where one is in life, prayer is available at all times. It is an opportunity and privilege to pray. Prayer is also a command, given

[8] Billy Graham. *The Faithful Christian: An Anthology of Billy Graham.* Compiled by William Griffin & Ruth Graham Dienert. (New York: McCracken Press, 1994) 144-145.

[9] John Wesley. *A Plain Account of Christian Perfection, #186. In John Wesley's 'A Plain Account of Christian Perfection: Annotated Edition.* By Mark K. Olson. (Fenwick, MI: Alethea, 2005), 235.

[10] James S. Stewart. *Walking with God.* (Vancouver: Regent College Publishing, 1996), 42.

for our own good. Like a gift, prayer should be received, utilized, and enjoyed. Like a weapon or shield, prayer should be used to resist temptation. Prayer is as essential to our spiritual life as eating is to our physical well being. We can choose to pray or choose to be spiritually malnourished. All healthy relationships require time, commitment, and intentionality. The same requirements apply to one's relationship with God because prayer is the chief means by which a person communicates with God.

Hindrances to Prayer

Despite understanding the value and benefits of prayer, Christians often encounter obstacles that prevent praying. Sin is the greatest obstacle to prayer. As we've discussed throughout this book, scripture defines sin as "falling short of the glory of God," and that all are guilty of sinning (Romans 3:23). Other than scripture, I think John Piper provides one of the best descriptions of sin that I have ever heard. According to Piper, sin occurs when:

The glory of God is not honored.
The holiness of God is not reverenced.
The greatness of God is not admired.
The power of God is not praised.
The truth of God is not sought.
The wisdom of God is not esteemed.
The beauty of God is not treasured.
The goodness of God is not savored.
The faithfulness of God is not trusted.
The promises of God are not relied upon.
The commandments of God are not obeyed.
The justice of God is not respected.

The wrath of God is not feared.

The grace of God is not cherished.

The presence of God is not prized.

The person of God is not loved.

The infinite, all-glorious Creator of the universe, by whom and for whom all things exist (Rom. 11:36), who holds every person's life in being at every moment (Acts 17:25), is disregarded, disbelieved, disobeyed, and dishonored by everybody in the world. That is the ultimate outrage of the universe. That is sin.[11] Everyone, including all Christians, will always have to deal with the desire to sin. We are lured and enticed by our own desires that often give birth to sin. Then sin gives birth to death (spiritual destruction, guilt, despair) and hinders our prayer life. Sin is pleasurable for a season, yet the consequences of disobedience can last much, much longer (James 1:12-15).

The Bible declares that humanity is incapable of producing anything good apart from God's intervention (Rom. 3:9-12). Therefore, both the desire and ability to pray are impossible without God's help. John Calvin begins his section on prayer in the *Institutes* by focusing on the depravity of man: "how destitute and devoid of all good things man is, and how he lacks aids to salvation."[12] As we discussed in the chapter about the devil, many people feel unworthy to approach God because of the guilt and shame that accompanies sin. Thankfully, even though we can do nothing on our own, we can turn to a sovereign God to meet our every need (John 15:1-11). When we realize our desperate need for God's forgiveness and grace, the proper response should be to ask for help. And because Jesus is our advocate and mediator, God will always hear and accept our prayers (1 John 2:11;

[11] John Piper. "The Greatest Thing in the World." www.desiringgod.org.
[12] Ibid.

1Tim. 2:5). Charles Spurgeon points out that there is hope for our lame, limping supplications because our faulty cries are not criticized by Christ.[13] By grace through faith every sinner is forgiven and can therefore approach God's throne of grace with confidence (Heb. 4:16). Focusing on Christ's victory over sin enables believers to live in victory instead of despair.

Sinners Becoming Saints

Apart from Christ and the biblical writers, perhaps no one has had a greater influence on Western Christianity than St. Augustine, bishop of Hippo (354-430). Yet Augustine was not always a "saint." In fact, prior to his conversion, Augustine lived for everything except God's glory. His autobiography, *Confessions*, is one of the most transparent and encouraging memoirs I have ever read. Reflecting upon his pre-conversion years, Augustine said, "I looked for pleasure, beauty, and truth not in God, but in myself and his other creatures. That search led me instead to pain, confusion, and error." Because of grace alone, Augustine realized his sin and offered a prayer of praise to his Savior: "You awaken and stir us so that only in praising you can we be content. You have made us for yourself, and our hearts our restless until they find their rest in you."[14] Thomas Merton also came to Christ after realizing the fact that there will always be a battle between one's flesh (sinful nature) and spirit:

> I had fallen asleep in my sweet security. I was living as if God only existed to do me temporal favors. Only when all pride, all self-love has been consumed in our souls by the love of God, are we delivered from the thing which is the subject of those torments. It is only

---

[13] Charles Spurgeon. *Power in Prayer*, 134.
[14] Augustine. *The Confessions.* (New York: Vintage, 1998), 1.20.

when we have lost all love of ourselves for our own sakes that our past sins cease to give us any cause for suffering or for the anguish of shame.[15]

Both Augustine and Merton realized the importance of confessing sin and turning to God for forgiveness and strength. It is important to confess sins to God, and also to the person who has been offended (James 5:16). Doing so removes guilt, clearing our consciences and our path to prayer. As a parent, I usually know when my boys have made mistakes, as well as the motive behind their actions. Regardless of their intentions, I am delighted when they come to me with their questions, frustrations, and apologies. In a similar yet far more intimate way, our heavenly Father longs to hear from us (Matt. 7:11). Despite our sin and feeble efforts, the Bible declares that God will forgive all who confess their sins (Rom. 10:9). Because of Christ's great love for us, and our faith in what he has done, like Augustine and Merton, we are both sinners and saints.

Turning Worry into Prayer

Worry can be another obstacle to prayer. Everyone worries at times, even though Jesus commands his children to trust Him (Matt. 6:25-33). There were times during college when I worried about my grades, work, relationships, faith, and future. I'll never forget a mentor's advice that helped me overcome my fears: "Having concern about life is not the same as worrying about life. Life has its challenges, but you need to realize that worrying is a choice." As we continued the conversation, I realized that the issue was not that I worried, but what I did with my worry. Jesus tells us that worry doesn't change or solve

---

[15] Thomas Merton. *The Seven Storey Mountain.* (New York: Hartcourt, 1998), Seven Storey Mountain, 322-323.

anything (Matthew 6:27). The personal breakthrough came when I chose to turn my worry into prayer. Each time I worried, I decided to pray and read the Bible. Two helpful passages for reflection are:

> You keep in perfect peace whose mind is stayed on you (Isa. 26:3). Cast your cares on the Lord and he will sustain you; he will never let the righteous be shaken (Ps. 55:22).

As I learned to share my burdens with the Lord instead of always feeling the need to go to others first, a couple of positive things happened. As time went on, I found myself worrying less and praying more. I also drew closer to God. Life has its challenges, but through prayer and scripture reading, God can replace our worry with peace and power.

A Holy Occupation

I've heard Christians tell me that they simply do not feel like praying. No one said it would be easy. In fact, prayer is hard. It takes time, effort, and commitment. Oswald Chambers, author of the best-selling devotional *My Utmost for His Highest*, defined prayer as "our holy occupation."[16] Those who despise work will likely not feel like praying either. Perhaps you realize the importance of prayer and want it to be a significant part of your life but simply have trouble getting started. The first step is to get started and not to give up.

I remember how unnatural it was when learning how to play the guitar. My fingertips hurt when trying to hold down the strings to play, and the whole process seemed awkward at first. Yet as I kept at it, my fingers became calloused, which alleviated the pain while playing. Before long, playing the guitar seemed more natural with each passing

---

[16] Chambers also wrote *Prayer: A Holy Occupation*, one of the most influential books on prayer I've ever read.

day. In subsequent weeks I was able to strike the chords with ease and began to find much pleasure in playing. In a similar way, prayer seems very unnatural when one first gets started, yet through commitment, perhaps even calloused knees, the process begins to become less like work, and more natural, spontaneous, and enjoyable. Richard Foster, author of the classic work, *Celebration of Discipline*, explains:

> We must never wait until we feel like praying before we pray. Prayer is like any other work; we may not feel like working, but once we have been at it for a bit, we begin to feel life working. A pianist may not feel like playing the piano, but once he plays, he feels like doing it. In the same way, our prayer muscles need to be limbered up a bit and once the blood-flow of intercession begins, we will find that we feel like praying.[17]

Whether we feel like it or not, we need to be governed by the Word of God, not our feelings. If obedience to God's scriptural mandates was determined by feelings, many people would never pray, much less have an intimate relationship with God. If we want to know God and his will for our lives, we must pray. If we want to become more like Christ, we must pray. The end of our labor in daily prayer should be to know Christ better. John Calvin claimed that failing to pray "would be of as little profit as a man to neglect a treasure, buried and hidden in the earth, after it had been pointed out to him."[18] Keep in mind, it is not about asking and receiving materialistic treasure, but realizing that every time we pray we are conversing with the Lord of all creation. When we understand this reality, our holy occupation becomes even more valuable and enjoyable.

[17] Richard J. Foster. *Celebration of Discipline: The Path to Spiritual Growth*. (San Francisco: HarperCollins, 1998), 45.
[18] Calvin. *Institutes*. (3.20.1)

God Hears Our Prayers

Some people do not pray because they doubt God will listen to their prayers. Some have asked, "Does God really hear our prayers?" The answer is absolutely yes, and if God was unmoved or unconcerned by our prayers then we're wasting our time.[19] Moreover, if God did not plan to listen to our prayers, why would he bother commanding us to pray? God not only commands us to pray, but he also promises to hear our prayers. James said, "Come near to God and he will come near to you" (James 4:8). Jesus said, "Ask and it will be given to you; seek and you will find; knock and the door will be opened to you. For everyone who asks receives; the one who seeks finds; and to the one who knocks, the door will be opened" (Luke 11:9-10). The sovereign Lord knows what we need before we ask him yet beckons us to pray (Matthew 6:8). When we realize that God delights in our prayers, prayer will become a delight. Think about who gives the promise—our Lord and Savior Jesus Christ, the Creator and Sustainer of all things. Why should we doubt his promise? Spurgeon said it best:

> When the Creator gives his creature the power of thirst, it is because water exists to meet its thirst. When he creates hunger, there is food to correspond to the appetite. When He inclines men to pray, it is because prayer has a corresponding blessing connected with it. If there is no answer to prayer, prayer is a monstrous absurdity. If it is indeed true that the effects of prayers end with the man who prays, then prayer is a work for idiots and madmen, not for sane people![20]

Luther said, "God commands prayer not to deceive or make fools out of us. Rather, God wants us to pray and be confident that we will

---

[19] Peter Kreeft. *Angels and Demons: What Do We Really Know About Them?* (San Francisco: Ignatius, 1995), 22.

[20] Charles Spurgeon. *The Power in Prayer*, 9-10.

be heard."[21] The reason why we are heard is because of the one who guarantees that we will be heard. Jesus said, "All authority in heaven and on earth has been given to me" (Matt. 28:18). The New Testament reveals God's expectation of our prayers. Three times in one passage, Jesus said, "*When* you pray (Matt. 6:5-7). On another occasion Jesus told his disciples to always pray so as not "to lose heart" (Luke 18:1).

Jesus promises that if we ask, he will listen and respond. Though his response may be different than our request, we can always trust that he will do what is best for his glory and our good. Luke said, "Consider the ravens: They do not sow or reap, they have no storeroom or barn; yet God feeds them. And how much more valuable you are than birds" (Luke 12:24). Commenting on this passage, Spurgeon said, "Now if God hears a strange, chattering, indistinctive cry as that of a raven, do you not think that he will also hear the rational and expressive prayer of a poor, needy, guilty soul who is crying to him?" Scripture and history reveal that the prayers of believers are always answered:

> Indeed, if you call out for insight and cry aloud for understanding, and if you look for it as for silver and search for it as for hidden treasure, then you will understand the fear of the Lord and find the knowledge of God (Proverbs 2:3-5).

God does not hear us because of the quality of our effort in prayer, but on the ground of our redemption through Jesus.[22] Therefore, Christians can be assured that God will always hear their prayers.

---

[21] Martin Luther. *Sermons on the Catechism.* ed. John Dillenberger. (New York: Anchor Books, 1962), 217.

[22] Oswald Chambers. *Prayer: A Holy Occupation.* ed. Harry Verploegh. (Grand Rapids: Oswald Chambers Publications, 1992), 19.

Yes, No, and Slow

Do you expect God to answer your prayers? Like much of life, the outcome of our prayers may be different than what we expect or desire. Some have asked, "What are we to make of the times where we diligently and sincerely prayed for something, and it didn't happen?" Rest assured, God always hears our prayers and will do what is best. This means that sometimes the answer to a particular prayer might be "no."

I've discovered that God will sometimes deny what we want in order to give us what we really need. If given everything we requested, we would probably be miserable. Someone once said that God is never late but rarely early. Sometimes the Lord will delay in responding to teach patience and trust. The prophet Daniel prayed and waited twenty-one days for God's response (Dan. 10:2-4). The Apostle Paul asked the Lord three times to take away the "thorn" that was plaguing him, yet God refused to grant his persistent prayer.

We must remember that God, who knows what is best in a way that we do not, may deny our specific requests for our own protection and good. If God doesn't seem to respond, it is because he has something better to give than what was requested. Make note of God's response to Paul's specific request about removing his burdens: "My grace is sufficient for you, for my power is made perfect in weakness" (2 Cor. 12:7-9). It is not that we should refrain from sharing our frustrations and pain with God but realize that our weaknesses can serve to remind us of our daily dependence on God no matter how well or poorly things seem to be going from our vantage point. Because God desires intimacy with us, is it possible that he could delay his response in order for us to pray more often? Think about it—without our wounds, frustrations, and needs, where might our focus and power be? There will be times in life when we ask God, "Why are you allowing this to happen to me?" Though an appropriate question, I've found it more useful to ask God, "What is it that you want to teach me through my circumstances?"

The Bible declares that, "God's ways are not our ways, and his thoughts are not our thoughts" (Isa. 55:8-9). Challenging circumstances often bring us closer to God. Though life can be hard and seem unfair, the key is to communicate with God through prayer. Our persistence in prayer shows both our confidence that God is our only hope and our belief that he will act in the best way and best time in response to our persistent pleas.[23]

Approaching the Throne of Grace in Faith with Confidence

We have looked at various hindrances to prayer and reasons why people do not pray. We have also been assured from scripture that God hears our prayers. Now let's look at the role of faith in prayer. Jesus tells us that if we pray in faith he will grant our requests according to his will (Matt. 21:22). James tells us that we should pray without doubting (James 1:6). Luther claimed that persons should never doubt the fact that God hears our prayers: "Do not leave your prayer without having said or thought, 'Very well, God has heard my prayer; this I know as a certainty and a truth.' That is what Amen means."[24] Puritan Thomas Watson claimed that "prayer that is faithless is fruitless."[25] Calvin said, "Faith grounded upon the Word is the mother of right prayer.[26] Scripture makes it very clear that "without faith it is impossible to please God, but anyone who comes to him

[23] John Piper. *What God Demands of the World.* (Wheaton, IL: Crossway, 2006), 108.

[24] Martin Luther. *Luther's Works, Volume 43: Devotional Writings.* ed. Gustav K. Wiencke. (Philadelphia: Fortress Press, 1968), 198.

[25] I.D. E. Thomas. *A Puritan Golden Treasury*, 213.

[26] Calvin, *Institutes*, (3.20.27).

must believe that he exists and that he rewards those who earnestly seek him" (Heb. 11:6). A. W. Tozer reminds us that, "Without faith there can be no approach to God, no forgiveness, no deliverance, no salvation, no communion, no spiritual life at all."[27]

Even though there will be times when we don't have the faith necessary to pray, Christ and the Holy Spirit will help us in our weakness (John 16:4-15; Rom. 8:26-34). Christ is our representative before God (Acts 7:55-56; Rom. 8:34; Eph. 1:20; Col. 3:1). The Apostle Paul reminds us that, "Christ Jesus, who was raised to life is at the right hand of God interceding for us, and in the same way the Spirit helps us in our weakness. During those times when we can't find the words or strength to pray, the Spirit intercedes for us with groans that words cannot express (Acts 7:55-56; Rom. 8:26-34; Eph. 1:20; Col. 3:1).

Though our prayers may differ in form, faith is the key component to their power.[28] When Jesus said, "according to your faith it will be done to you" (Matt. 9:29), he did not mean that we get whatever we ask for, or just because we have faith and are obedient to pray that God will give us exactly what we ask of him. Motive means everything. It requires faith not only to believe that God will hear us, but also to believe that God will work in and through our prayers. Let us never forget that prayer is not just asking God for things, nor should it be about bargaining with God or trying to manipulate God to get what we desire. Rather, prayer should be about communicating with God, getting to know God better, and asking for his will to be done in our lives. Oftentimes people get this backwards. How often do we pray only for physical healing while completely ignoring the fact that spiritual healing is far more important? How often do we pray for

[27] A.W. Tozer. *The Pursuit of God.* (Camp Hill, PN: Wing Spread Publishers, 2006), 80.
[28] Spurgeon, 19.

the salvation of lost people so that they may be more pleasant to be around, instead of praying for their salvation and spiritual growth? At times we've made prayer much more about ourselves than God's glory. Though sometimes difficult, we must always pray for God's glory and will to be done. When we pray in this manner, God's faithfulness will be proven time and time again.

Time to Pray

Many of us feel as though we don't have the time to pray, yet this is exactly why we should pray more than we do. It is not coincidental that all godly persons throughout the ages were people of prayer. Martin Luther once stated, "I have so much business I cannot get on without spending three hours daily in prayer."[29] John Wesley devoted at least two hours every day to fervent prayer.[30] Jonathan Edwards once mentioned:

> I spent most of my time thinking of divine things, year after year; often walking alone in the woods and solitary places for meditation, soliloquy, and prayer, conversing with God. It was always my manner, at such times, to sing forth my contemplation. I was almost constantly in prayer, wherever I was. Prayer seemed to be natural to me, as the breadth by which the inward burnings of my heart had vent.[31]

Edwards was very intentional about his prayer life, and he took time to pray. Despite caring for a congregation and large family, Edwards spent twelve to thirteen hours a day in his study, which included

---

[29] Richard Foster. *Celebration of Discipline: The Path to Spiritual Growth.* (San Francisco:HarperCollins, 1998), 34.

[30] Ibid.

[31] Excerpt of Jonathan Edwards's *Personal Narrative* quoted by Philip E. Howard in "A Biographical Sketch of the Life and Work of Jonathan Edwards." *The Life and Diary of David Brainerd.* ed. Jonathan Edwards. (Grand Rapids: Baker House, 1989), 16.

many hours of prayer. David Brainerd was a student and friend of Edwards and also a missionary to Native Americans in the New England area during the pre-Revolution era. He lived in a shack in the wilderness and was often plagued by illness and fatigue, yet Brainerd found extraordinary pleasure in his daily pursuit of God. Numerous diary entries reveal his commitment to prayer: "I never feel comfortable, but when I find my soul going forth after God. If I cannot be holy, I must necessarily be miserable forever."[32] Brainerd longed to be alone with God and often devoted entire days to prayer. Another entry reads, "In the morning, spent about two hours in prayer and meditation, with considerable delight." It was not uncommon for Brainerd to devote entire days in communion with the Lord—"I set apart this day for fasting and prayer."[33]

Thomas Merton often spent two to three hours in daily prayer as well.[34] What can we learn from these testimonies? That it will be impossible to have a right relationship with God, much less serve as we should, unless we are willing to spend time conversing with God through prayer. It is not a matter of having enough time, for we all have been granted twenty-four hours each day. It has to do with how we manage the time we've been given. Think about how you spend the time God has given you. We all make time for the people and things that are important to us. Regardless of how busy or tired we are, we find time to engage in the relationships and activities that we value most. It is all about priorities, and we have to be intentional about our time of prayer.

---

[32] Ibid., August 15, 1743 journal entry.
[33] Ibid., April 20, 1743 journal entry. See also November 10, 1743.
[34] Merton, 428.

Starting the Day off Right

Is there a particular time of day that you've set aside for prayer? I'm not a morning person but have come to learn from scripture the importance of praying before my feet hit the ground each day. Mark's Gospel reveals that Jesus got up very early in the morning to pray (Mark 1:35). The Psalmist said, "My voice shall you hear in the morning. O Lord; in the morning will I lay my requests before you and wait in expectation" (Ps. 5:3). As the Psalmist declared, and theologian Dietrich Bonhoeffer concurred, "the first thought and the first word of the day belong to God."[35] Reading, meditating on scripture and praying should serve as the foundation of each day. The Old Testament prophet Ezekiel said, "In the morning the word of the Lord came to me" (Ezekiel 12:8). Charles Spurgeon claimed that "it should be our rule never to see the face of men before first seeing the face of God, because the morning watch anchors the soul that it will not very readily drift far away from God during the day."[36] It has been said that the most important meal of the day is breakfast, for it provides us with the energy needed to start the day. Similarly, beginning each day with prayer is also beneficial.

George Whitefield, arguably the greatest evangelist in history, claimed that the power of his preaching resulted from his time in prayer. His diary reveals that he often prayed early in the morning, again at noon, and just before retiring for the day.[37] Twentieth-century preacher A.W. Tozer also understood the importance of starting each day in communion with God. Reverend Bobby Moore shares a remarkable account:

[35] Dietrich Bonhoeffer. *Life Together.* (New York: Harper, 1954), 29.
[36] Bobby Moore. *Your Personal Devotional Life.* (Southaven, MS: The Kings Press, 2004), 4.
[37] Ibid, 14.

When an acquaintance of mine was called to preach in Chicago, A. W. Tozer called him and said, "This city is a devil's den. It is a very difficult place to minister the Word of God. You will come up against much opposition from the enemy. If you ever want to pray with me, I am at the lakeside every morning at five-thirty. Just make your way down and we can pray together." Not wanting to bother the great man as he was seeking the Lord, the new minister did not immediately accept his offer. But one day he was so troubled that he made his way very early to the lakeside, about six o'clock, only to find God's servant prostrate upon the sand. Needless to say, he did not disturb him.[38]

The key for each believer is to strive for ongoing conversation with the Lord, while always seeking the best opportunities to pray. Calvin exhorted believers to set specific times to pray: "When we arise in the morning, before we begin daily work, when we sit down to a meal, and when we are getting ready to retire."[39] We would be wise to ask God for guidance and provision in the morning, pray for strength, wisdom, and discernment throughout the day, and give thanks for all God has provided in the evening.

Praying Continually with Thanksgiving

The Bible declares, "Be joyful always; pray continually; give thanks in all circumstances, for this is God's will for you in Jesus Christ" (1 Thess. 5:16-18). Unfortunately, we fail to obey this command when we allow circumstances to dictate our prayer life. Though scripture tells us to pray continually, many times we turn to prayer as a last resort after we have exhausted all other means to remedy our problems. There are times when we would rather bring our concerns to others instead of

---

[38] Ibid, 4.

[39] Calvin, *Institutes,* (3.20.50).

God. There are other times when we refuse to pray because we are un-grateful. If we don't sense a need to pray, what does that say about our understanding of prayer and closeness to the Lord? How can we pray continually, and with thanksgiving, regardless of our circumstances? The Apostle Paul faced persecution and imprisonment for following Christ, yet gave the following charge to Christians living in Philippi:

> Rejoice in the Lord always. I will say it again: Rejoice! Let your gentleness be evident to all. The Lord is near. Do not to be anxious about anything, but in everything, by prayer and petition, with thanksgiving, present your requests to God. And the peace of God, which transcends all understanding, will guard your hearts and your minds in Christ Jesus (Philippians 4:4-7).

God is honored in the manner due him when he is acknowledged as the author of all blessings.[40] Every day is a gift, and every prayer should reflect our thanksgiving to God for all he has provided each day (food, shelter, health, clothing, friends, family, and many more blessings). Because God is the giver of all good things, praying demonstrates both our thanksgiving for and reliance upon God's provision (James 1:17). Consider all that you have been given, and give thanks to God through prayer.

Praying with Humility

Humility is also an important component of successful prayer, for the very act of prayer demonstrates humility. The opposite of humility is pride, and if we think we are not prideful, we might need a dose of humility. I remember not wanting to pray aloud in front of others because I cared too much about what people would think about my prayers. I also recall times in life when I refused to pray because I was

---

[40] Calvin, *Institutes*, (3.20.28).

ungrateful or didn't think I needed God's help. Praying with humility has characterized godly persons throughout history. Puritan William Secker stated that, "Pride is the sinner's torment, but humility is a saint's ornament."[41] Another Puritan, Thomas Brooks, wrote:

> God cares not at the elegance of your prayers, to see how neat they are; nor at the geometry of your prayers to see how long they are; nor at the arithmetic of your prayers to see how many they are; nor at the music of your prayers, nor at the sweetness of your voice, nor at the logic of your prayers; but at the sincerity of your prayers.[42]

Even though some people may be impressed by our prayers, God never will be. I've often been reminded of this truth when listening to the simple prayers of children, as they freely share with God whatever comes to mind.

Not only have I been guilty of trying to impress people with my prayers, but I have also tried to impress people by trying to serve in my own strength instead of relying on God. There have been other times when I was so busy trying to serve the Lord that I failed to utilize God's strength that was needed to serve. In each instance, my pride was the root of the problem.

I've often wondered about how pride has hindered my spiritual journey. It reminds me of the time I watched my seven-year-old create a race track in a sandbox, only to experience frustration due to a large rock preventing smooth passage for his little cars. I offered to help, but he refused. After ten minutes of digging, kicking, and trying to remove the rock, my son's lip quivered as he started to cry. He then said, "Dad, I'm so mad about this rock messing up my race track, and I can't move it." I then said, "Son, have you thought about asking me for help?" He said, "No, because I didn't think I needed

---

[41] Quoted in Thomas. *A Puritan Golden Treasury*, 147.
[42] Ibid, 212.

it." I have often let obstacles distract me and stubbornly refused to ask for God's assistance. It was a joy to remove the rock and watch my son's frustration go away. In a similar way, God is always nearby, knows our needs, and delights when we ask for help.

Meditating on and Praying Scripture

Your prayer life will often be a reflection of your view of and trust in God. The better your knowledge of God, the more intimate and powerful your prayers will be.[43] Because we come to know God best through the scriptures, the most fruitful prayers are rooted in the scriptures. There are no better words to guide our thoughts and prayers than the very words of God. This is why reading, memorizing, savoring, and praying the scriptures are so important to one's spiritual journey.

What comes to mind when you think about the word *meditation*? Unfortunately, the word has taken on a negative connotation for years, but when one understands the value of meditating on the words of God, one's prayer life often becomes richer. Meditating on scripture enables us to claim the promises of God and verbalize them back to him. Meditating on scripture can enable us to witness how God forgave sinners, met needs, performed miracles, and overcame sin, death, and hell. It also reminds us that nothing can separate us from God's love.

I am convinced that we need to hear from God by reading the Bible before allowing God to hear from us through prayer. If you will spend time reading and meditating on scripture, I believe you will discover that your prayer life will become richer in the process. Because reading God's words can encourage, convict, challenge, and transform our thinking, it makes sense to read scripture before praying. Because

[43] Timothy Keller. *Prayer: Experiencing Awe and Intimacy with God.* (New York: Dutton, 2014), 49.

our thoughts are often scattered, even when trying to pray, meditating on scripture can place our attention on God's words instead of our wandering thoughts. It is certainly wise to say a prayer just before reading scripture, but communion with God is often richer when one allows God to start the conversation. John Cassian, a contemporary of Augustine in the fourth century, commented on the importance of preparing to pray:

> The praying spirit is shaped by its earlier condition, so therefore before we pray, we must hasten to drive from our heart's sanctuary anything we would not wish to intrude on our prayers.[44]

This is why reading the Bible prior to praying can transform our thought process in preparation to pray. Since we often don't know what to pray, why not read scripture before praying? Reading and meditating on scripture will inevitably lead to prayer because God speaks to us through the divinely inspired words of the Bible. Martin Luther prayed parts of scripture throughout his life:

> If I have had time and opportunity to go through the Lord's Prayer, I do the same with the Ten Commandments. I think of each commandment as, first, instruction, which is really what it is intended to be, and consider what the Lord God demands of me so earnestly. Second, I turn it into thanksgiving; third, a confession; and fourth, a prayer.[45]

Believers of every generation have realized the value of meditating on scripture. Below are some suggestions that might be helpful to you.

---

[44] John Cassian. *Conferences.* trans. Colm Luibheid. (New York: Paulist Press, 1985), 102-103
[45] Luther, *Works: Devotional Writings* II, 200.

Suggestions on How to Meditate on Scripture:

1. Select a passage of scripture.

2. Plan to use a journal or paper to write out your thoughts and questions as you read, reflect, and pray. You may also plan to write out your prayers.

3. Ask God to impact your mind and heart through your reading.

4. Try meditating quietly or choosing to read and pray aloud in order to focus better on communion with God. Either way, try reading the verse or passage slowly and repeatedly.

5. As you read, think about context. Who is the author? Who is being addressed? What are the setting and theme of the story? You may want to utilize a study Bible, Bible dictionary, or Bible commentary for insight about context. Imagine what the author and persons in the story were thinking or feeling.

6. Think about how you might apply God's truth revealed in the passage to your daily life and witness.

Though the Psalms and Gospels are often most conducive to meditation, you can focus on other parts of scripture as well. In order to provide you a sense of what this might look like, I have provided a couple passages I've meditated on in the past, as well as the reflections I wrote in my prayer journal.

> You will keep in perfect peace him whose mind is steadfast, because he trusts in you (Isa. 26:3).

> My reflections: God, forgive me for worrying about things I cannot control. Thank you for always being in control of all things. Thank

you for reminding me through this passage written by the prophet Isaiah centuries ago that if I focus on you, you will give me peace. Help me to trust you today, Lord.

For I am convinced that neither death nor life, neither angels nor demons, neither the present nor the future, nor any powers, neither height nor depth, nor anything else in all creation, will be able to separate us from the love of God that is in Christ Jesus our Lord (Romans 8:38-39).

My reflections: God, I am grateful for your never-ending love and provision. Forgive me for being distracted by temptation and the temporary things of this world. No matter what challenges I may face today, Lord, I know that nothing can separate me from your love and grace. Please help me model your love and grace for everyone you bring into my path today.

Praying the Psalms

The Psalms, which were originally sung, have helped generation after generation to pray. The Psalms reveal the character of God and his creatures. The full range of human emotion is contained in the Psalms—sorrow, joy, pain, thanksgiving, worry, anger, frustration, fear, doubt, hope, peace, and praise. They reveal how God relates to his creatures and how we are to relate to him. The New Testament has explicit references to the psalms, including the instance when Jesus quoted a Psalm while dying on the cross (Ps. 22:1). The Apostle Paul encouraged the believers at Ephesus to sing the Psalms (Eph. 5:18-19). The Psalms were quoted frequently by the church fathers and have played an important role in the lives of great leaders over the centuries. St. Augustine knew the Psalms by heart, as reflected throughout *The Confessions*. During the last ten days of his life, Augustine wanted to be left entirely alone. His only request was to have the Psalms of David copied out and hung on the walls of his room. Augustine's desire was to spend his final days gazing at and praying the Psalms.[46] Dietrich Bonhoeffer read the Psalms every day for years, and once said, "I know them and love them more than any other book."[47] Given that there are 150 psalms, choosing to read and pray five psalms per day would enable one to make it through the entire book of psalms in a month. In addition to the Bible, the majority of hymnals and prayer books contain portions of the Psalms and can therefore be utilized to aid one's time of prayer as well.

Free and Formed Prayers

If you spend enough time hearing a person pray, you will realize that everyone prays both free and formed prayers. The *Book of Common Prayer* prescribes many beautiful, powerful prayers for believers to pray, and most of them are tied directly to scripture.[48] Some may object to the idea of praying a prescribed prayer, but people who insist that all prayers must be "new," unstructured, or spontaneous are simply mistaken. Millions of Christians have experienced the richness of praying formed prayers for centuries. The Lord's Prayer is one example. Though Catholics, Anglicans, and those of the Greek Orthodox tradition frequently utilize formed prayers, Christians of all traditions say the same prayers before congregations, meals, and bedtime on a regular basis. What matters more than the choice between praying free or formed prayers is the substance of the prayers (being biblically based) and the motive and condition of the heart

---

[46] Augustine. *The Confessions.* Quoted in the preface by Patricia Hampl. (New York: Vintage, 1998), xxvi.

[47] Dietrich Bonhoeffer. *Letters & Papers from Prison.* ed. by Eberhard Bethge. (New York: Touchstone, 1971), 40.

[48] In addition to prescribing prayers for many special occasions and times throughout the liturgical year, The *Book of Common Prayer* contains prayers translated from the Latin by 16th century theologian Thomas Cramner that Anglicans utilize each Sunday of the year.

of the one praying. Just like praying freely, using prescribed prayers can enrich our communication with God. Below are examples of two prayers (a prayer of confession and a prayer of thanksgiving) found in the *Book of Common Prayer* that could be useful during your daily time of prayer:

> Most merciful God,
> we confess that we have sinned against you
> in thought, word, and deed,
> by what we have done,
> and by what we have left undone.
> We have not loved you with our whole heart;
> we have not loved our neighbors as ourselves.
> We are truly sorry and we humbly repent.
> For the sake of your Son Jesus Christ,
> have mercy on us and forgive us;
> that we may delight in your will,
> and walk in your ways,
> to the glory of your name, Amen.
>
> Almighty God, Father of all mercies,
> we your unworthy servants give you humble thanks
> for all your goodness and loving-kindness
> to us and to all whom you have made.
> We bless you for our creation, preservation,
> and all the blessings of this life;
> but above all for your immeasurable love
> in the redemption of the world by our Lord Jesus Christ;
> for the means of grace, and for the hope of glory.
> And, we pray, give us such an awareness of your mercies,
> that with truly thankful hearts we may show forth your praise,
> not only with our lips, but in our lives,
> by giving up our selves to your service,
> and by walking before you
> in holiness and righteousness all our days;

through Jesus Christ our Lord,
to whom, with you and the Holy Spirit,
be honor and glory throughout all ages. Amen.[49]

There are many prayers recorded in the New Testament that could also be utilized during your daily time of prayer (Eph. 3:14-20; Heb. 13:20-21; 1 Pet. 1:3-5 and Jude 24-25.

Following the Lord's Example

To pray rightly is a rare gift, and Jesus provided the perfect example.[50] Prayer was a way of life for Jesus. The occasions for his prayers were many and varied. He prayed in the early morning and also late at night (Matt. 1:35; 14:23). He frequently prayed alone and sometimes with others (John 6:15). He prayed during one of his miracles (John 11:41-42). He prayed while blessing meals (Luke 9:16, 24:30; Matt. 15:36; 26:26-27) and also to bless and heal people (Matt. 19:13-15; Luke 27:50). Before selecting his twelve disciples, Jesus "went out to a mountainside to pray, and spent the night praying to God" (Luke 6:12). Since it was necessary for Jesus regularly to spend time during the day and night praying, we must "let Christ's example be a spur inciting us to amend our leisurely approach to prayer."[51]

Prayer preceded major decisions in Jesus's life, as evidenced throughout the New Testament. His decision to leave Capernaum and preach "in the other cities" also followed the prayer in "a lonely place" (Mark 1:35; Luke 4:42-43). He prayed in the Garden of Gethsemane the night before his crucifixion (Luke 22:41-42). While hanging on

---

[49] *The Book of Common Prayer.* (New York: Church Publishing Incorporated, 1979). These two prayers are recited every day by millions of Christians around the world.

[50] Calvin, *Institutes,* (3.20.5).

[51] John Calvin. *Sermons on the Beatitudes: Five Sermons from the Gospel Harmony, Delivered in Geneva in 1560.* trans. by Robert White (Edinburgh: Banner of Truth Trust, 2006), 8

the cross Jesus prayed for the Lord to forgive his persecutors (Luke 23:34).

Not only did Jesus lead by example, he also instructed his disciples specifically how to pray. When asked how to pray, Jesus responded with what has come to be known as "the Lord's Prayer" (Matt. 6:9-13; Luke 11:1-4):

> Our Father, who art in heaven, hallowed be thy Name.
> Thy kingdom come, thy will be done, on earth as it is in heaven.
> Give us this day our daily bread, and forgive us our tresspasses,
> as we forgive those who trespass against us. And lead us not
> into temptation, but deliver us from evil. For thine is the king-
> dom, and the power, and the glory, for ever and ever. Amen.[52]

By understanding and praying the Lord's Prayer we are allowing the very words of King Jesus to guide our prayer. Commenting on the significance of the Lord's Prayer throughout his life, Luther declared, "It is the very best prayer, even better than the psalter, which is so very dear to me." Luther also said, "Every time you are tempted you should go running to the Lord's Prayer."[53] Calvin viewed the Lord's Prayer as the pre-eminent model, and Jesus himself as the person through whom persons must always pray: "Our prayers have no access to God unless Christ, as our High Priest, having washed away our sins, sanctifies us and obtains for us that grace from which the uncleanness of our transgressions and vices debars us."[54] After all, Christ is at the right hand of God as the Mediator who intercedes on our behalf (Rom. 8:34; 1 Tim. 2:5). This being the case, the Lord's Prayer should be part of our daily lives.

---

[52] *The Book of Common Prayer.* (New York: Church Publishing Incorporated, 1979), 54.
[53] Luther, *Works: Devotional Writings II,* 200.
[54] Calvin, *Institutes,* (2.15.6).

Practical Prayer

Along with Bible study, prayer served as the foundation upon which many of the most faithful Christians built their lives. History provides numerous examples of leaders who knew that the effectiveness of their teaching, preaching, and ministries were inseparably linked with prayer. Obeying the command to pray is absolutely essential for a Christian to have a healthy, growing relationship with God. One of the most amazing aspects of prayer is that the Creator and Sustainer of the entire cosmos always hears us when we pray. Though we are in the presence of God at all times, it is important to regularly schedule times of prayer. If you are not intentional about prayer, it will never become a priority in your life. This may mean being selfish about your time with God. Barring an emergency, try not to let anyone or anything keep you from your designated time with God. Jesus said to love the Lord and your neighbor as yourself (Luke 10:27). Without reading God's Word and praying you will not grow in your love for God, and therefore not love yourself or others as you should. Just as you would write down an important appointment, write down the time you plan to meet with the Lord, whether it be on your phone, iPad, digital or printed calendar.

In addition to being intentional about scheduling times to pray, you should also be intentional about having a designated place to pray, especially one free of distractions. Just as you would devote undivided attention when meeting with someone really important, you should turn off your television, phone, computer, or whatever else may distract from your daily meeting with the Lord. God desires your undivided attention, and it will be for your good to provide it.

Jesus once said, "For where two or three gather in my name, there am I with them" (Matt. 18:20). There are few things more important than praying with others. This being the case, consider having another person or group to pray for and with on a regular basis.

It has been said that a dull pencil remembers more than a sharp mind. No matter how great your memory, you will sometimes forget prayer requests. Keeping a prayer list helps us to remember who and what to pray for, and it also serves as a way to look back and chart answered prayers. You might also consider making a list of things you are grateful for. After making a list, give thanks to God through prayer.

In conclusion, I would like to share a personal story that helped me realize the importance of prayer. I had never really thought much about writing down prayer requests until attending seminary. During one of my first courses, which was a five-day winter term, my professor began each class period inviting students to share prayer requests. Since I had spent my undergraduate years at a secular institution, sharing prayer requests publicly or keeping a prayer list seemed a little weird even though I was now attending a seminary. Besides, this was a theology class, and I was ready to learn about theology and doctrine, not how to have some type of counseling session where people could share their problems. During the first day of class I was a little surprised to hear a dozen students mention prayer requests, and even more so when the professor took time to write down each petition. This guy was serious about prayer! After ten minutes and several glances at my watch, I wondered if we would ever get on with learning about the Bible.

After the professor asked for the thirteenth time if anyone else had a prayer request to share, a long pause ensued before a student on the front row partially stood up and faced the class. His large hearing aids and slurred speech made me realize that he was hearing impaired. He apologized for his reluctance to share his need. He also apologized for his speech impediment and then mentioned that normally he didn't have so much trouble hearing, but that his hearing aids were old and no longer working very well. Literally in tears, he mentioned that he felt so helpless and discouraged about becoming the preacher God called him to be because he could not hear and therefore could not learn what was necessary during his time of training. The professor asked him the cost of new hearing aids, to which my fellow student said would be about $4,000. I was broke, like most other seminary students, but really wanted to provide monetary support for my class-mate. The professor then placed his hand on the student and asked us to join him in prayer.

At that moment I really felt convicted about having been so lax about prayer, and initially bothered by the teacher devoting so much of class time to taking prayer requests. From that day forward I made the commitment to write down prayer requests so that I would re-member to pray for specific people and needs. The very next day our professor began class by asking the hearing-impaired student to stand beside him. The professor put his hand on the student's shoulder and said to the class:

> Yesterday our brother in Christ was willing to share his need because something was keeping him from learning and doing his best for God. God knew before the foundation of the world what each of our needs would be today. We have prayed for our brother, and God has done what he planned to do all along (Matthew 6:8).

> How blessed we are to have been given the gift of prayer, and to have approached the throne of grace with confidence together. I received a call yesterday from a friend who was in town on business. Over dinner I mentioned to him the specific prayer request that was shared in class yesterday. I am overjoyed to share with you the fact that last night I was given a check for $4,000 so that our brother can get the hearing aids he needs in order to be the preacher God has called him to be.

I had been a Christian for many years before realizing the importance of prayer, and making prayer a priority in my daily life. I hope that you will learn to take advantage of this opportunity as well.

Questions for Discussion:

1. How do you define prayer?

2. Who guarantees that our prayers will be heard?

3. Is prayer part of your life? Why or why not?

4. Are you satisfied with your prayer life? If not, how might it be improved?

5. Are you satisfied with your knowledge of scripture and how you are applying it during your times of prayer? If not, how might it be improved?

6. Why is praying the Lord's Prayer important?

7. Can you think of people and needs in your life to pray for? Consider writing them down in a prayer journal, as a reminder to pray, and also in order to look back on the ways in which God may have responded to your prayers.

For Further Reading:

The Book of Common Prayer. New York: Church Publishing Incorporated, 1979.

Oswald Chambers. *Prayer: A Holy Occupation.* ed. Harry Verploegh. Grand Rapids: Oswald Chambers Publications, 1992.

Timothy Keller. *Prayer: Experiencing Awe and Intimacy with God.* New York: Dutton, 2014.

Charles Spurgeon. *The Power in Prayer.* New Kensington, PA: Whitaker House, 1996.

A.W. Tozer. *The Pursuit of God.* Camp Hill, PN: Wing Spread Publishers, 2006.

BEFORE YOU LEAVE

I'll never forget watching a 2005 interview of Tom Brady, the multi-millionaire, multi-Super-Bowl-winning quarterback of the New England Patriots. When asked about all of his success on and off the football field, Brady provided a response that most people would not expect:

> Why do I have three Super Bowl rings and still think there is something greater out there for me? I mean, maybe a lot of people would say, "Hey man, this is what it is, I've reached my goal, my dream, my life." Me, I think *God, there's got to be more than this.* I mean this can't be what it is all cracked up to be, I mean, I've done it, I'm 27, and what else is there for me? The interviewer then asked Brady, "What's the answer?" Brady responded, "I wish I knew. I wish I knew."[1]

If people are honest, deep within their hearts exists a longing for something more. We all know the experience of desiring something

---

[1] https://www.youtube.com/watch?v=-TA4_fVkv3c "Tom Brady on Winning: There's Got to Be More Than This."

so badly and really believing it would make us happy, only to obtain it, and then realize that the satisfaction didn't last.

C.S. Lewis once said, "If I find in myself a desire which no experience in this world can satisfy, the most probable explanation is that I was made for another world."[2] Lewis was exactly right. You and I were made for another world, and it is called eternity. Recall Jesus's words:

> Do not store up for yourselves treasures on earth, where moths and rust destroy, and where thieves break in and steal. But store up for yourselves treasures in heaven, where moths and rust do not destroy, and where thieves do not break in and steal. For where your treasure is, there your heart will be also (Matthew 6:19-21).

In other words, people can choose to focus on temporary or eternal treasures. We chase after temporary pleasures all of the time, even though we know the fleeting nature of these pursuits. How many things you found to be so valuable at the time you received them (trophies, awards, clothes, toys, gadgets, etc.) are now in a closet, attic, drawer, or trash dump? It all comes down to your perspective about life and death.

I used to teach at a university that borders a national military cemetery, and throughout the day numerous funeral processions could be seen from the balcony of the building in which I taught. On many occasions, one of my colleagues stopped students between classes and announced, "Everyone, look over there at that hearse leading the procession of cars to the funeral! You'll never see a U-Haul moving truck behind the hearse!" When we die, nothing can be taken with us.

This reality causes some to ignore death and focus only on the

---

[2] C.S. Lewis. *Mere Christianity.* (San Francisco: HarperCollins, 2001), 52.

here and now. "Live it up; make the most of it. You only go around once, so enjoy the one life you've been given" are common refrains in society today. I agree that we should enjoy life, focus on the moment, and make the most of each day. But I have also found myself asking the question, "If this world is all there is, what would be the ultimate reason for living?"

People have approached this question in a variety of ways. For those who do not believe in an afterlife, there is nothing more important than obtaining all this world has to offer. One may be fortunate enough to live to be 80 or 90 and accomplish all of their dreams, but when the inevitability of death draws closer, the possibility and hope for something beyond one's funeral starts to press its case more forcibly. I've found that very few people, if challenged to think deeply about the matter, actually believe there is nothing beyond the grave.

I developed a greater appreciation for the value of time and concept of eternity during a conversation with the oldest person I have known. As we arrived for the birthday celebration for my wife's grandmother, I couldn't wait to ask her for advice about how to live to be 102 years old. When I asked her for the secret, she said, "one hundred and two years is a long time, but compared to eternity it seems very short. When you live for the Lord, everything else will fall into place. I'd also recommend always keeping an eye on eternity." Clearly, she knew that even the longest life is brief in comparison to eternity. She also understood the value of the time she had left. She died within days of her 103rd birthday.

Throughout the New Testament and the history of the church, people have warned that the end is near. The skeptic might say, "Well, we are still waiting." Fair enough, but for you, me, and every generation, death will arrive at some point. So, in that sense, the end is near. The sudden, tragic deaths of Kobe Bryant and eight others resulting from a helicopter crash reminded all of us about the preciousness of time and unpredictability of life. The global coronavirus pandemic of 2020 caused most of the civilized world to ponder the possibility of death. The end of your time on earth may be sooner than you think, and it is getting closer with each passing moment. Based on what the Bible teaches, death is the beginning of eternity to be spent either in heaven or hell. Christians also believe that Jesus Christ will return to earth one day in bodily form, and this too is closer with each passing moment. When Jesus returns, the "end" will be the beginning of the final judgment and our time in eternity. If that is true, its consequences are enormous—too enormous for us to dismiss without careful investigation.

Even if you don't believe in God, the Bible, or eternity, you still need to come to terms with how to live the rest of your life in light of your own mortality. After all, death is the most permanent part of life. Most people don't know how to respond to it, especially when it arrives too soon for people we know and love. Few want to talk or think about it, but eventually each of us will face it. We're reminded of this reality every time we attend a funeral.

I have a friend who helps people plan funerals, even for those who are young and in good health. It's a little creepy, I know. Though I wasn't interested in his services, his offer of assistance caused me to contemplate what my funeral might look like and how long I might live. Given that life expectancy in America is around seventy-eight years, my life is statistically likely to be halfway over. Have you ever thought about how long you might live? Simply subtract your age from seventy-eight and you will get an idea of the number of years you might have left, that is, if you live to reach the national average.

Because life is precious and unpredictable, the way we approach each day matters more than most people realize. The Bible states,

"You do not even know what will happen tomorrow. What is your life? You are a vapor or mist that appears for a little while and then vanishes" (James 4:14). Time is precious, and you and I are not promised tomorrow. No matter how long you may live, at some point your heart and breathing will stop, and you will be gone. Then what? What will matter once you have died? What do you think people will remember and say about you?

Certainly, those who knew you best and were most impacted by your life will show up for your funeral. They'll be handed a program featuring one of your better pictures on the cover, along with the dates of your birth and death. Those assembled will likely hear your eulogy, some type of sermon, and a few stories about your life and accomplishments. Afterward, the mourners will have a nice meal, hear a few more stories about you, and then move on with their lives. You will be gone, and though some will think about you often, many will seldom think about you again. It's a sobering thought.

Like most people, I don't like to think about death, but I believe it is important for us to acknowledge that each day we are getting closer to this inevitable reality. Death is the last thing on the minds of most young people, especially when college and career are on the horizon. Regardless of our stage in life, we can dread death, ignore it, or come to peaceful terms with it. Though the idea of death is unpleasant, it is possible to have peace about it, especially if you know Jesus and live your life in light of the gospel. You don't have to fear life or death when you know that Christ is alive. The Bible declares that, "If the Spirit of him who raised Jesus from the dead is living in you, he who raised Christ from the dead will also give life to your mortal bodies through his Spirit who lives in you" (Romans 8:11).

How we view Jesus is vitally important, and what we do with that belief matters most. There are really only three choices regarding the identity of Jesus—he was either a blasphemer, which is what he was accused of being and why he was eventually killed; he was crazy; or he was and is God.[3] Jesus should have been deemed crazy for claiming to be God if he were merely a man.

The difference between Christianity and all other religions or belief systems is how one views Jesus Christ. Founders of other religions claimed to teach the truth, but Christ claimed to be the truth. Jesus said, "I am the way, the truth and the life, and no one comes to the Father except through me" (John 14:6). Jesus is the way to God because he is God. No other religious leader in history could make and back up that claim. In fact, no founder of any other major religion ever claimed to be God. Jesus is one of a kind because he is the one true God.

Becoming a Christian is not about obeying rules, jumping through hoops, or raising a hand during a church service in order to receive salvation. Being a Christ follower is so much more than trying to be saved from hell or going to heaven. When one truly embraces Christ as Savior and repents of his or her sins, that child of God immediately enters into a personal relationship with the Creator and Sustainer of the universe. It is a relationship more powerful than any other, and it lasts for eternity. The Bible also declares that, "If you confess with your mouth, Jesus is Lord, and believe in your heart that God raised him from the dead, you will be saved. For it is with your heart that you believe and are justified, and it is with your mouth that you confess and are saved. Anyone who trusts in him will never be put to shame" (Rom. 10:9-11).

Everyone bases their life and future on something. Without the

---

[3] C.S. Lewis explained in *Mere Christianity* that Jesus was either the Lord, a liar, or a lunatic. Anyone claiming to be God would either be lying, crazy, or actually God. The New Testament reveals that Jesus claimed to be God. Those who disagreed eventually killed him for blasphemy (claiming to be God). His resurrection was the ultimate miracle that proved he really was God in the flesh. There are only three choices regarding the identity of Jesus: call him a liar, crazy, or God.

resurrection of Jesus Christ, Christianity would not exist, and we would have no hope. The Apostle Paul tells us, "If it is preached that Christ has been raised from the dead, how can some of you say that there is no resurrection of the dead? If there is no resurrection of the dead, then not even Christ has been raised. And if Christ has not been raised, our preaching is useless and so is your faith" (1 Cor. 15:12-14). Through the cross and resurrection of Jesus Christ, our sins are forgiven, and we are promised eternal life. There is nothing you have done or can ever do to make God love you any more or any less than he always has. If you are a Christian, give thanks, and praise God for his amazing grace that you've received. If you are not yet a believer, I encourage you to make it a priority to investigate who Jesus claimed to be, and what happened as a result of his life, death, and resurrection.

Even the most skeptical non-Christian historians cannot explain how Christianity came to be the largest and most influential religion in the world, especially given the fact that it began in an obscure town, amid a powerful empire that should have prevented its inception and continuation. Apart from the story being true, there is no way to explain how a small group of ordinary Christ followers who lived under enormous scrutiny and persecution could have overcome the odds and blossomed into a movement that has billions of adherents to this day. If Jesus was not raised from the dead, Christianity would have died on the cross with him two thousand years ago.

It's been said that the older we get, the faster time seems to go. People tend to realize the preciousness of time when certain seasons or chapters of life come to an end. Whether it is the end of high school, college, a vacation, or career, most of us tend to pause and reflect before moving on to the next chapter. The death of a loved one usually brings things into proper perspective. It was certainly the case for me. My father died a couple years ago following a lengthy battle with Parkinson's disease. The last time I saw him was really special. I knew that each visit to the nursing home could be my last. As I arrived, my father was sitting in his wheelchair just outside his room as if he knew I was coming. I remember pushing him down the hallway to a secluded place so that we could enjoy uninterrupted conversation. I never knew how lucid he might be, but I figured it would be nice to sing a couple of my dad's favorite hymns, like "A Mighty Fortress is Our God," or "Great is Thy Faithfulness." He loved hymns, but unfortunately couldn't remember any of the words. Singing wasn't meant to be that day, but we did enjoy a few hours of conversation.

As I began pushing my father down the long hallway to his room, my steps became shorter and slower, for it was always hard to leave. Once we arrived at his room, I picked up my dad and tucked him in to bed. The best way I knew to say goodbye was to pray. It was a blessing hearing my dad recite part of the Lord's Prayer with me. After saying "amen," and "I love you Dad," it was time for me to leave. Facing the door, with my back turned to my father, I just stood there in silence, praying and reflecting on our time together that day as well as other good memories we'd shared over the years. All of a sudden, my father started singing, "Jesus loves me, this I know, for the Bible tells me so." There was nothing more important for him to remember or for me to hear.

ACKNOWLEDGMENTS

I must start by thanking James Kinnard and the amazing team at the Useful Group for their expertise and professionalism. Thanks for your creativity, Robbie Hall, Carson Cheatham, and Miranda May. I am grateful for your editorial help, Matt Rogers. Rachel Poel, your hard work, attention to detail, and guidance made this entire project enjoyable and successful. I also want to thank my unofficial editors, Kendall Conger and Mike Rainwater, whose keen insight and helpful suggestions always kept me moving in the right direction.

I am very grateful for Tim and Jessica Capps, Jim and Laura Crenshaw, David and Amanda Chambers, Jay and Lynn Easterling, Andy and Hope English, Patrick Hamner, Chris and Heidi Hendricks, Walter Hussman, Larry and Candace Mallard, Jule and Alisa Smith, and Larry Stone —for believing in me and the message God put on my heart. This book would not have been completed without you. To the students, parents, faculty, staff, administration, and Board of St. David's School, I am grateful for your encouragement that made the dream of writing this book become a reality. Special thanks to Kevin Lockerbie and Jonathan Yonan for your support.

Thanks to President Tim Gibson and The King's College community for getting behind this project. What God is doing through you in the cultural capital of the world is truly remarkable.

I am also indebted to President Adam Wright and Chancellor Gary Cook of Dallas Baptist University. I am grateful for your leadership and the investment you have made in my life. To my students and the rest of the DBU family, I am also grateful for your prayers and support over the past twenty years.

Thanks to the group of dear friends who read manuscripts, provided helpful comments, and walked closely with me throughout the entire project— James Heinrich, Brody and Julie Hildebrand, Blake Holmes, JT McPherson, Steve Noble, and Kell Peterson.

I also want to thank those who read specific drafts or chapters and provided invaluable insight along the way— Bruce Ashford, David Billingslea, Paul Blaze, Ray Casey, Ryan Collier, Don and Lucy Dancer, Ross Douthat, David Eagle, Elizabeth Feeney, Wes Gristy, Sarah and Bellamy Harden, Nicholas Harris, Matt Hoehn, Mark Hijleh, David Johnson, Steven, Susan and Riley King, Mike Licona, Jack Lloyd, Matt and Jamie Martin, Tony Merida, Graham Michael, Joe Matos, Justin Nalls, Dan Panetti, Garrett Raburn, Jake Rodgers, Kerry and Beverly Rouser, Steve Sharkey, Shelette Stewart, Dana and Stephanie Simpson, Ardyn Smith, Warren Smith, Chris Stratton, Mike Strauss, Dan Sturdevant, Mark and Lauri Towns, Madi Vanarthos, Peggy Wehmeyer, Jackie Welsh, Madison Welsh, and Ray Williams.

Other friends who contributed in important ways include: Sherry Ball, Cliff and Anna Benson, Dan Bitar, Blair Blackburn, Clint and Susan Bond, Kevin Brown, Dan and Grace Casey, Jim Cianca, Andy and Cathy Coats, Josh Copeland, Neale Davis, George and Elizabeth DeLoache, Mark and Gina Doskocil, Stu Epperson, Jerry and Becky Freeman, Dan Gibson, Dave Harding, Desi Henk, Bill Henry, Bonny Herrington, Jon and Michelle Homeister, Todd Humphrey, Greg Kelm, Danny and Karen Kennemur, Blake Killingsworth, Joe and Sarah Knott, Jeff and Abbey Land, Don and Miriam Leshnock, David Luckey, Mark Martin, Sarah Merriman, Eric Metaxas, Billy and Donna McClatchey, Warte Moore, Paul and Jane Murphy, Dave Newton, Michael Noto, Jim and Amy Pannell, Matt Perman, Wayne and Billie Ann Peterson, Bruce and Mary Jo Pierce, Frank and Renee Pierce, Ralph and Leigh Powell, Blake Rankin, Steve Rankin, Elizabeth Rieker, Paul and Diana Risk, Tom and Angie Rhoads, Blair Robinson, Bridget Rogers, Brandon Smith, Scott Shaw, Leigh Stallings, Jason and Amanda Steele, Jerry Stoltz, Ron and Jeanne Stringfellow, Nathaniel Sullivan, Ed Thomas, Michael Toscano, the Vick family, Bill and Jill Vanarthos, James and Laura Vann, David and Kris Welsh, Robert Whitfield, Travis Whitfill, Michael and Heather Wick, Ben Wickel, Ben Wood, Gene and Telitha Wright.

I thank God for the spiritual mentors and academic leaders whose words and actions have always made me want to be a better Christ follower. Grace and peace to you Wayne McAfee, Scott Blair, Glenn Kreider, Gary Starnes, Mike Williams, David Naugle, Grant Wacker, Billy Abraham, and Ken Keathley.

Special thanks to another group of close friends whose love and support over many years have meant more than you will ever know —Darren and Mendy Autry, Robby Clay, the FBCCH and FBOC families, Wes and Abbie Gristy, Jason and Teresa McCord, John and Brandee Miles, Bob and Donna Moncrief, Chris and Shauna Reilly, Steven and Ashley Smith.

To my sister and brother-in-law, Tamara and Adam Mergener, and nieces Tadam and Tarin, thanks for taking special care of mom and dad during their twilight years, and for supporting me along the way. To Mike, Carol, Chad, and Ryan Cull, I am grateful for you as well. I also want to thank my in-laws, Ron and Patricia Page, for your love and on-going encouragement. To the extended Cull, von Helms, and Page families, blessings to you.

And to my best friend, Caroline—none of this would have been possible without your unconditional love, never ending prayers and support.

Made in the USA
Middletown, DE
25 September 2020